Wine and *Cheese*

of *France*

Frank Artigaud

GREMESE

Original title: Fromages et Vins de France
Copyright © 1998: Open Door Limited
Translation: Christine Stone

Layout: Mireille Palicot
Photographer: Jean-Paul Paireault
Editor: Dominique Artigaud
Editorial Services: P.E. Fogarty
Editor English Edition: Christine Stone

Photocomposition: IM.A.G.E. - Rome
Printed in Singapore by Imago

Copyright © 1998 GREMESE EDITORE s.r.l.
Via Virginia Agnelli, 88 - 00151 Rome
Fax 39/6/65740509
E-mail: gremese@gremese.com
Internet: www.gremese.com

CONTENTS

INTRODUCTION

Try this test. Buy a good wine, a Médoc for example. Taste it. Next, help yourself to a piece of Roquefort and then, right after that, end your tasting session with another glass of the same Médoc. Surprise! It doesn't taste the same. In fact, you may even feel that it has left an unpleasantly insipid taste in your mouth. Yet, both the wine and the cheese were excellent. You will have just experienced the results of mismatching wine and cheese.

Every wine has a cheese to go with it. This is even more true the other way round: every cheese has a wine to go with it.

Let us then go on a quest for the perfect combinations, from the most traditional to the most daring, in order to learn how to match different varieties of wine and cheese like a professional wine taster would.

'When entertaining a guest, one has the duty to ensure their happiness for the whole of their stay', used to say Brillat-Savarin, perhaps the most famous French gourmet, author of *The Physiology of Taste* (1826). He also added that a meal without cheese was like a beautiful woman with only one eye; would the good one be sufficient to gauge the quality of the beverage.

France is renowned all over the world for the quality and the variety of her wine and cheese. She produces more than three hundred types of cheese, thirty-two of which are classified *Appellation d'Origine Contrôlée* (Controlled Appellation of Origin or A.O.C.). As far as wines are concerned, there are over two hundred and fifty classified names, reputed to be the best in France.

Vins Délimités de Qualité Supérieure (Limited Wines of Superior Quality or V.D.Q.S.), on the other hand, are quality wines ranking just below A.O.C. status.

The ability to taste a really good cheese and find the wine that goes with it is part of the art of good living most deeply rooted in French tradition.

Nowadays, white wines are increasingly used to accompany the cheese tray. Nothing compares to combining a Sauternes with some Roquefort or a pink Champagne with some Chaource.

Gastronomy is the art of successful combinations, the art of enhancing a wine through the accompanying cheese. It is about making sure that the time your guests spend sitting round your table eating will be bliss for them.

BORDEAUX

This generic appellation *groups all wines from the vineyards of the Gironde region that comply with a variety of regulations (such as the mix of grape varieties, alcohol, yield per acre) and according to their specific character. There are seven generic* appellations: Bordeaux, Bordeaux Claret, Bordeaux Rosé, Bordeaux Supérieur, Bordeaux Claret Supérieur, Bordeaux Supérieur Rosé and the sparkling Bordeaux Mousseux.

THE COMMUNAL OR REGIONAL APPELLATION

This may cover only one district (Médoc, Haut-Médoc, Graves, Entre-Deux-Mers) and have a specific appellation, *according to the official classification* (Grand Cru *or great growth,* Premier Cru - *first growth,* Cru Bourgeois - *ordinary growth). There are forty such* appellations.
For red wines:
- the Médoc and Haut-Médoc districts, with six communal appellations: Margaux, Moulis, Listrac, Saint-Julien, Pauillac, Saint-Estèphe.
- Pomerol, Lalande-de-Pomerol, Fronsac, Canon-Fronsac and Néac.
- Saint-Émilion, with six satellite appellations: Saint-Georges-Saint-Émilion, Montagne-Saint-Émilion, Parsac-Saint-Émilion, Lussac-Saint-Émilion, Puisseguin-Saint-Émilion, Sables-Saint-Émilion.
- Graves, Graves Supérieur and Pessac-Léognan.
For white wines:
- Sauternes, Barsac, Cérons, Entre-Deux-Mers, Graves-de-Vayres, Sainte-Foy-Bordeaux, Cadillac, Loupiac, Sainte-Croix-du-Mont, Côtes de Bordeaux Saint-Macaire.
For red and white wines:
- Côtes de Blaye, Premières Côtes de Blaye, Côtes de Bourg, Premières Côtes de Bordeaux, Bordeaux Côtes de Castillon, Bordeaux Côtes de Francs.

Bordeaux wines are famous throughout the world. The Bordeaux wine region is the largest in France and boasts a wide variety of vines. The region's 250 000-acre vineyard area produces about thirty specific appellation *wines (Margaux, Saint-Émilion, Pomerol, Sauternes, etc....) from over 5000 estates, or* châteaux, *2000 of which are especially representative.*

The Cos d'Estournel estate at Saint Estèphe

St-Christoly-Médoc

Lesparre-Médoc

St-Seurin-de-Cadourne

ST-ESTÈPHE

CÔTES DE BLAYE

MÉDOC   PAUILLAC

ST-JULIEN

St-Laurent-
et-Benon

Blaye

LUSSAC
MONTAGNE
ST-GEORGES
PARSAC
PUISSEGUIN

LISTRAC
MOULIS

CÔTES DE BOURG

MARGAUX

Bourg

Cantenac

St-André-
de-Cubzac

LALANDE-
DE-POMEROL

FRONSAC
CANON-
FRONSAC

POMEROL

CÔTES DE FRANCS

HAUT-MÉDOC

Libourne

ST-ÉMILION

CÔTES DE CASTILLON

Le Pian-Médoc

St-Loubès

Castillon-la-Bataille

GRAVES
DE VAYRES

Ste-Foy-
la-Grande

Bordeaux

Mérignac

ENTRE-
DEUX-MERS

Pujols

Pessac

STE-FOY-
BORDEAUX

Talence

Créon

Rauzan

CÔTES-DE-
BORDEAUX

Targon

Léognan

Sauveterre-de-Guyenne

Portets

CADILLAC

GRAVES

LOUPIAC

STE-CROIX-
DU-MONT

Monségur

GRAVES

Podensac

CÉRONS

CÔTES-DE-BORDEAUX-
ST-MACAIRE

BARSAC

Langon

SAUTERNES

MÉDOC

GRAPE VARIETIES

CABERNET SAUVIGNON
MERLOT
CABERNET-FRANC
PETIT VERDOT
MALBEC (OR COT)
CARMENÈRE

Opposite, the cellars of Ducru-Beaucaillou at Saint-Julien

MARGAUX

According to its most enthusiastic devotees, this excellent, full-bodied red wine takes a few years to mature.

The Château Margaux estate stands out from the rest. Its vineyards, classified *Premier Cru*, stretch over 150 acres and produce a remarkably fine wine. The Margaux *appellation* covers four neighboring towns.

MOULIS

The distinctive character of Moulis-en-Médoc wines depends mainly on the quantity of limestone in the soil, which exceeds by far the regional average.

The Moulis *appellation* covers 865 acres of vineyards, divided among Moulis and six neighboring districts. It also includes several *Crus Bourgeois*. The most renowned Moulis wine is undoubtedly Château Chasse-Spleen.

LISTRAC

At one of the highest points of Haut-Médoc, a stone's throw from the forest, Listrac vineyards grow on pebbly soil, down gentle slopes which produce beautifully ruby-colored red wines.

The *appellation* comprises some *Crus Bourgeois Supérieurs*, including the very highly reputed

Château Clarke and Château Fourcas-Dupré.

PAUILLAC

With three world-famous wines and eighteen *Crus* classified in 1855, Pauillac is indisputably the wine capital of Médoc.

SAINT-ESTÈPHE

Saint-Estèphe wines owe their distinctiveness to the slightly damp clay subsoil on which the vineyards grow. These wines are sturdy, with a rich bouquet and fruity in youth. They differ considerably from one estate to another.

SAINT-JULIEN

This small *appellation* is one of the greatest by wine quality standards. It is one of the five world-famous A.O.C. of the Haut-Médoc district. It includes eleven *Grands Crus* classified in 1855. A Saint-Julien is more robust than a Margaux, but just as delicate; it lacks the concentration of a Pauillac, but has the same sturdy character. It is halfway between the two, just like its geographical location.

HAUT-MÉDOC

The Haut-Médoc produces top-quality wines, among which there are five classified growths and a remarkably vast array of *Crus Bourgeois*.

In order to qualify for the Haut-Médoc *appellation*, wines must be made from cabernet sauvignon, cabernet franc, cot and petit verdot grapes.

Haut-Médoc red wines derive their charme from their complex bouquet. They are well-balanced, with a rich flavor and considerable finesse. In their youth, traces of tannins are often detectable. However, they age remarkably well.

MÉDOC

At the northernmost point of the Gironde region, the Médoc zone includes fifteen districts qualifying as Médoc A.O.C. Requirements concerning the type of vine and alcohol of Médoc *appellation* wines are identical to the ones applying to Haut-Médoc.

Vineyards produce deep ruby-colored, vigorous, tannic wines, which evolve considerably with age.

The alchemy between land and climate here is less subtle than in the Haut-Médoc district.

CHARACTERISTICS

These wines are delicate, with a good bouquet, discreet and fine and some of them can age up to a hundred years. Pauillac is robust.
Margaux has great finesse and great allure.
Saint-Éstèphe is tannic and very aromatic.
Saint-Julien boasts a very pleasant aroma, combining spices and vanilla.
Moulis is very robust and colored.
On the palate, Médoc is a rich, full-bodied, very pleasant wine with race.

GRAVES

Bottle of Château Haut-Brion, first Grand Cru Classé *at Pessac.*

GRAVES

This region derives its name from the French word for "gravely", used to define a pebbly terrain mixed with sand and clay, producing different wines according to the proportions of the mix.

The Graves A.O.C., which until 1987 used to include Pessac and Léognan, stretches between the river Garonne and the forest of the Landes, from the southern edge of Bordeaux to Langon, leaving out the Sauternes region.

Let us start our journey at Saint-Morillon, where we find the old estate of Château Camarset, the vineyards of Château Belon surrounded by pine trees and finally Château Claron, where legend has it that Napoleon I and his troops once drank the whole harvest in a single afternoon.

Traveling down from Cabanac-et-Villagrains, through the forest, we come to Landiras and Château d'Arricaud, where it is possible to enjoy a delightful view of the Garonne and the Sauternes hills . The road continues through Budos and Léogats, round the edge of the Sauternes region, down to Mazères, the southernmost point of the Graves zone, where white and red wines of very distinctive character are made. Portets and its surroundings bear witness to the wine-growing history of the region, especially at Chateaux Crabitey - whose land was turned into vineyards by the Franciscan monks - and Château de Portets, which prides itself on having given hospitality to Napoleon I. Castres-en-Gironde boasts some *châteaux* of historical importance too, all producers of Graves: Ferrande, Saint-Hilaire and Sansaric. The journey comes to a magnificent end at the gates of the region's most beautiful *château*, La Brède.

PESSAC-LÉOGNAN

The Pessac-Léognan *appellation* created in 1987 covers the old *appellations* of Graves-Pessac and Graves-Léognan. It includes about ten districts situated south of Bordeaux, where all the Graves named in the 1953 and 1959 classifications are produced.

Château Haut-Brion at Pessac.

Haut-Brion, the only estate classified in 1855, is one of the jewels in the crown of the Bordeaux region. Château Laville-Haut-Brion produces white wine and features among the first five classified *Premiers Crus* of Graves. Château Pape-Clément, one of the oldest wine-making properties of the region, is named after Pope Clement V, who removed the papal seat from Rome to Avignon.

Château Carbonnieux, where both white and red wines are made, belonged to the clergy for a long time. Legend has it that in the 18th century they exported their white wine to faraway Turkey. One may well wonder how they managed to cross those borders, considering that Islamic law forbade the consumption of all fermented drinks. The shrewd monks sold their product under the name 'Carbonnieux sparkling water'. It was as simple as that.

WHICH CHEESE?

CAMEMBERT
FOURME
ROQUEFORT

Blending of a Graves

CHARACTERISTICS

The white wines are nervy, robust and with bouquet.
The reds share the same characteristics but they are sounder, with a silky and delicate finish.
They have a strong nose, dominated by a red fruit aroma and a woody finish.

11

SAUTERNES
BARSAC AND CÉRONS

GRAPE VARIETIES

SÉMILLON
SAUVIGNON
MUSCADELLE

Opposite, *Château Yquem*, Premier Grand Cru.

In the Sauternes area, vineyards grow on a land where silica, clay and limestone create a unique combination which no other soil can equal.

What is more, harvesting is especially thorough, since grape berries are picked one by one as they reach the over-ripeness needed for vinification. The harvesting process may therefore continue for as long as eight weeks.

It is also important to note that both the sugar and alcohol in this wine come solely from fermentation of the must. This explains why white Sauternes is so unique. It has a golden color and boasts some exceptional qualities developed through aging, from which it benefits immensely. Sauternes wines, of which Château d'Yquem was named *Premier Cru* in 1855, are the pride and joy not only of the Bordeaux region, but of France herself.

BARSAC

This *appellation* covers, besides Sauternes, the districts of Preignac, Fargues, Bommes and Barsac. Barsac wines can use either the Barsac or the Sauternes *appellation*.

CÉRONS

Cérons, bordering Barsac, makes its white wine from the same grapes as Sauternes and follows the same procedures of selective picking when the grapes go beyond full ripening. Cérons is very

fine and elegant, less viscous than Sauternes, with more fruit and nerve.

Part of the harvest becomes dry or *demi-sec* white wine, fruity and with full color. This *appellation* covers Cérons and part of the Podensac area, on the banks of the river Garonne, and extends to the district of Illats.

WHICH CHEESE?

ROQUEFORT

CHARACTERISTICS

Sauternes is an exceptional viscous wine boasting a unique aroma ranging from dried and ripe fruit to flowers.
Cérons has a good structure and a bouquet which develops harmoniously.

13

SAINT-ÉMILION

GRAPE VARIETIES

MERLOT
CABERNET-FRANC
CABERNET-SAUVIGNON

Saint-Émilion is a remarkably well preserved medieval village, producing wines with a lovely color which are full bodied and robust. The *appellation* area stretches over 14 000 acres, including the vine-

The cellars of Château Beauséjour-Bécot.

yards of Saint-Émilion and seven neighboring districts: Saint-Christophe-des-Bardes, Saint-Etienne-de-Lisse, Saint-Hippolyte, Saint-Laurent-des-Combes, Saint-Sulpice-de-Faleyrens, Saint-Pey-d'Armens and Vignonet.
In 1977, the old area of the Sables-Saint-Émilion *appellation*, situated on Libourne territory, was added to the list. Saint-Émilion wines differ according to the varied composition

of the district's soil and subsoil. A main distinction is made between the wines produced on the hillsides and those made on the plateau.
The official classification of Saint-Émilion wines, first drawn up in 1954, lists eleven *Premiers Grands Crus* and sixty-three *Grands Crus*. Château Ausone and Château Cheval Blanc are the two most highly ranked estates.

SAINT-ÉMILION'S SATELLITE *APPELLATIONS*

Five districts north of Saint-Émilion proper have their own *appellation*, and their names are often hyphenated with Saint-Émilion.

LUSSAC-SAINT-ÉMILION

Lussac-Saint-Émilion produces on its hillsides a wine which is colored and robust, with some finesse.
The most renowned *châteaux* are Lyonnat, Bellevue, Lussac, Lion-Perruchon and Vieux-Chênes.

PUISSEGUIN-SAINT-ÉMILION

The vineyards of Puisseguin-Saint-Émilion, growing on stony hillsides, produce wines which are long-lived, meaty, colored and robust. The most quoted estates of the *appellation* are the *châteaux* of Les Lorets, Teillac, Roc-de-Boissac and Teyssier.

MONTAGNE-SAINT-ÉMILION

Montagne-Saint-Émilion is made in the largest of the satellite *appella-*

tions. The wines made on the hillsides are more powerful and colored than those made on the plateau; they are rather supple, full bodied and light. The *châteaux* of Montaiguillon, Des Tours, Corbin, Roudier and Négrit are reputed to be the best growths.

PARSAC-SAINT-ÉMILION

Parsac-Saint-Émilion vineyards grow on the hillsides and produce wines with good bouquet, though a touch less robust than their neighbors. Producers often sell them under the label of Montagne-Saint-Émilion, as they have been legally allowed to do since 1972.

SAINT-GEORGES-SAINT-ÉMILION

Saint-Georges-Saint-Émilion is one of the best satellite *appellations.* Its robust, full bodied wines, with their truffle bouquet, will keep particularly well.

After Château Saint-Georges, which produces a wine with breeding, the *châteaux* of Saint-André-Corbin, Saint-Georges-Macquin, Tourteau and Samion are also worth mentioning.

CHARACTERISTICS

These are generous wines, with a powerful impact on the mouth, warm and of a deep red color.
They are long-lived wines.

15

LIBOURNE

MERLOT
CABERNET-FRANC
CABERNET-SAUVIGNON

The Libournais vineyards are situated on the right bank of the river Dordogne, stretching out on both sides of the town of Libourne.

To the east of the town, they include the areas of Pomerol, Lalande-de-Pomerol and Saint-Émilion, which extends into the secondary plots of Côtes-de-Castillon - enjoying its own A.O.C. - and Côtes de Francs. To the west, there are the zones of Fronsac and Canon-Fronsac. This region produces both white and red wines, although only the latter have been given *appellation* status.

FRONSAC – CANON-FRONSAC

Fronsac is a medieval town towering over the river Dordogne, which has long been famed for its wines. It was the Duke of Fronsac who made Bordeaux wines fashionable at the court of King Louis XV.

The Fronsac A.O.C. includes Fronsac and six neighboring districts: La Rivière, Saint-Michel-de-Fronsac, Saint-Germain-La-Rivière, Saint-Aignan, Saillans and Galgon. The wines made in Fronsac, notably on the Canon hillsides, are entitled to the Canon-Fronsac *appellation*.

POMEROL

It would be excessive to say that Pomerol is made from iron. How-

On the right, harvesting in the Pomerol region.

ever, the original character of this prestigious wine is largely due to the iron oxide found in the subsoil of a small vineyard covering about 1700 acres. Pomerol wines have only recently started to be appreciated; up to the last century, they were mistaken for Saint-Émilion.

To this day, however, although Château Pétrus enjoys a worldwide reputation, Pomerol still has no official classification. In spite of this lack of official recognition, connoisseurs have long established a hierarchy of Pomerol wines, indisputably dominated by Château Pétrus.

What unique qualities this superb wine possesses. The vineyard where it is made is certainly rather small (27 acres), like the *château* with its turquoise windows nicknamed 'the doll's house'. This wine derives its qualities from a clay-rich subsoil, on which lies a thin layer of gravel, although the work of the wine-growers also plays an important role.

Yields are restricted for two reasons. First, because the vines they used are old and second because fermentation is prolonged by aging the wine in new vats for over two years.

LALANDE-DE-POMEROL

Lalande-de-Pomerol, located north of Pomerol and Néac, between Pomerol and Montagne-Saint-Émilion to the east, makes very similar wines to Pomerol, on a vineyard covering about 2200 acres.

WHICH CHEESE?

CAMEMBERT
BRIE
PONT-L'ÉVÊQUE

A hundred-year-old Cabernet Franc vine stock.

CHARACTERISTICS

Pomerol is a very generous, very sturdy wine, with a bouquet rich in aromas. Lalande-Pomerol is generous, supple and mellow. Canon and Canon-Fronsac are meaty, colored and fruity. They are generally long-lived wines.

17

ENTRE-DEUX-MERS

ENTRE-DEUX-MERS

From a strictly geographical point of view, Entre-Deux-Mers is a strip of land between the rivers Garonne and Dordogne - hence the name 'between two seas'. The border of the Gironde region forms the base of the ensuing triangle.

Ripe berries.

Vineyards are a fixed feature of the landscape of this pretty, undulating region. However, the Entre-Deux-Mers A.O.C. status is enjoyed only by the white wines produced in the *appellations* of Cadillac, Loupiac, Sainte-Croix-du-Mont, Côtes-de-Bordeaux-Saint-Macaire, Graves-de-Vayres and Sainte-Foy-Bordeaux. Nine districts of the Targon area are allowed to use the combined *appellation* Entre-Deux-Mers Haut-Benauge, named after the Benauge castle, a fortress towering over the area.

GRAVES-DE-VAYRES

This *appellation* is restricted to the small area of Graves on the left bank of the Dordogne, facing Libourne. About 1250 acres of vineyards divided between Vayres and Arveyres produce aromatic and supple red wines which evolve quite rapidly, as well as sweet white wines - the production of which has been decreasing over the last few years - and fresh and fruity whites. They are essentially wines to be drunk young.

SAINTE-FOY-BORDEAUX

This *appellation* lies at the edge of the Entre-Deux-Mers plateau, bordering the Bergerac region. It comprises pleasant, robust red wines, mellow and supple whites and dry white wines.

CADILLAC

This small village of the Bordeaux region does not owe its name to the famous American cars. In fact, it is rather the other way round. The American town of Detroit, where these cars are made, was founded by Mr. Lamothe-Cadillac. Cadillac A.O.C. applies to mellow or viscous white wines with a minimum of 13 percent alcohol.

The vineyard only covers about 250 acres spread over eighteen districts. Not far from Cadillac stands the imposing castle of the Dukes of Epernon, which now hosts the *Connétablie de Guyenne*, a wine-growing brotherhood whose members watch over the fate of the region's white wines.

LOUPIAC

These are mainly sweet white wines, made following the same regulations as those applying in the Sauternes region. They resemble the wines of Sainte-Croix-du-Mont. The best vintages of mellow wines are long-lived.

SAINTE-CROIX-DU-MONT

This *appellation* covers a group of sweet white wines made in plots where the Sauternes production regulations apply.

Here, the best sweet wines of the right bank of the Garonne are produced. They reach maturity after three to four years of aging.

CÔTES DE BORDEAUX SAINT-MACAIRE

This *appellation*, just south of the Premières Côtes de Bordeaux area, covers about 125 acres, divided among eleven districts.

This fairly small vineyard produces mellow, original and rather fine white wines.

WHICH CHEESE?

ROQUEFORT

CHARACTERISTICS

They are very harmonious wines, with a pleasant nose and a full bodied flavor, strongly marked by sauvignon grapes. The aromas are best appreciated in their youth.

19

LES CÔTES

GRAPE VARIETIES

CABERNET-FRANC
CABERNET-SAUVIGNON
MALBEC
MERLOT

Above, the port of Blaye.
Opposite, stainless steel fermenting rooms.

PREMIÈRES CÔTES DE BORDEAUX

These vineyards grow on varied subsoils and stretch from the top to the bottom of the hillsides, curling around the right bank of the river Garonne, from Sainte-Eulalie to Saint-Maixant. The *appellation* includes red and white wines produced in thirty-seven districts, of which Cadillac, Loupiac and Sainte-Croix-du-Mont are entitled to a specific *appellation*.

CÔTES DE BLAYE

A large vineyard extends around Blaye, the fortified town built by Vauban, stretching north to Saint-Ciers-sur-Gironde and east to Saint-Savin. This green area covers three *appellations* listed in 1936. The Blaye *appellation*, also called 'Blayais', covers red and white wines largely resembling their neighbors, although they are subject to more lax production rules.

CÔTES DE CASTILLON

These vineyards, right next to Saint-Émilion, grow on the steep slopes of the hills at the border of the Dordogne region.
Bordeaux Côtes de Castillon wines satisfy the criteria set for Bordeaux Supérieur. The *appellation* area covers the districts of Castillon-la-Bataille, Bièves-Castillon, Saint-Magne-de-Castillon, Les Salles, Saint-Gènes-de-Castillon, Monbadon, Saint-Philippe-d'Aiguille and Sainte-Colombe.

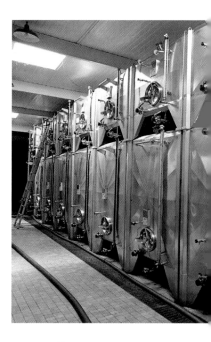

CÔTES DE FRANCS

This small vineyard, just north of Côtes de Castillon, produces red wine similar to Bordeaux Côtes de Castillon. Here too, the wine is made according to the regulations applying to Bordeaux Supérieur. The Bordeaux Côtes de Francs *appellation* covers Francs, Saint-Cibard, Les Salles and Tayac.

CÔTES DE BOURG

The right bank of the river Dordogne, where it joins the Garonne, is embellished with mountain-like

slopes, which have earned this region the nickname of 'little Switzerland of the Gironde'. Production of sweet white wine is modest, while the reds enjoy a very good and well-deserved reputation.

WHICH CHEESE?

CAMEMBERT
BRIE

Above, vinification of Merlot.

CHARACTERISTICS

Côtes de Bourg wines are full bodied, colored, robust and sturdy.
Côtes de Castillon and Côtes de Francs are very pleasant, rich wines with a lot of bouquet. It may take some time for the tannins to drop out.

21

BURGUNDY

The Burgundy wine-growing region stretches down from Chablis to the Côte d'Or, which includes Côte de Nuits and Côte de Beaune, and spreads over the Côte Chalonnaise and the Mâconnais districts down to the Beaujolais region, on the border with Lyon. This area of more than 75 000 acres is planted with chardonnay grapes, used to produce white wines, and with pinot noir, the great variety dominating red wines, with the exception of the Beaujolais region, where the white-juiced gamay noir à jus blanc is prevalent.

Below, the Hospices of Beaune.

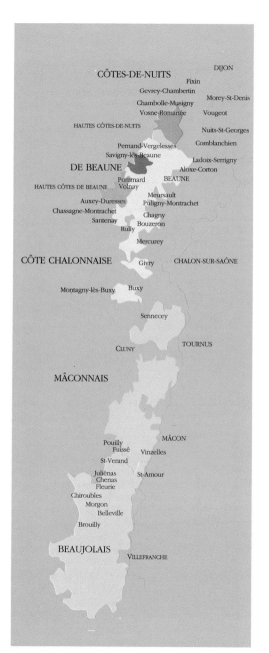

Burgundy's classification system is divided into four main levels.

THE REGIONAL APPELLATION

It is applied to all the wines produced in the region and may be followed by a reference to the type of wine, as in the case of aligoté wine.

THE SUB-REGIONAL APPELLATION

It applies to more restricted areas, such as Bourgogne-Hautes Côtes de Beaune, Mâcon...

THE COMMUNAL APPELLATION

This appellation is granted to some individual disticts of the region, such as Meursault, Pommard, Fixin...

THE SUB-COMMUNAL APPELLATION

This applies to small vineyards locally known as climats or crus (growths). The vineyards can also be classified as Grand Crus. There are thirty-one classified Grands Crus in the whole region.

THE BURGUNDY APPELLATION

Red and rosé wines are generally made from pinot noir and pinot gris grapes, except for the Yonne district, where the césar and the increasingly rare tressot grapes may be added to the blend. Chardonnay (also called beaunois or aubaine) and pinot blanc are used for white wines. These are blending wines containing at least 10 percent alcohol for the reds and 10.5 percent for the whites.

BOURGOGNE ORDINAIRE AND BOURGOGNE GRAND ORDINAIRE

The red and rosé wines must not contain less than 9 percent alcohol. They are made from pinot noir and pinot gris grapes and from césar and tressot in the Yonne district. White wines, which have a minimum of 9.5 percent alcohol, may be a blend of chardonnay, aligoté, Burgundy melon and sacy, which is only used in the Yonne district.

BOURGOGNE PASSETOUTGRAIN

This red wine must have at least 9.5 percent alcohol. Pinot grapes make up one third and gamay the remaining two thirds of the blend.

BOURGOGNE ALIGOTÉ

Chardonnay grapes may be added to the aligoté variety up to a maximum of 15 percent of the blend. These white wines have 9.5 percent alcohol.

CRÉMANT DE BOURGOGNE

This is made according to the traditional method for sparkling wine used in Champagne, and is made from first-rate grape varieties (pinot noir, pinot gris, pinot blanc and chardonnay) and second-rate ones (aligoté, melon, gamay noir à jus blanc).

CHABLIS

GRAPE VARIETIES

CHARDONNAY

On the right, a Chablis vineyard.

Sic transit gloria mundi... Every year, eighty to a hundred million gallons of wine using the name Chablis are produced throughout the world. However, the vineyards on the banks of the small Serein river - at about 60 miles from Dijon - only yield 2 500 000 to 4 000 000 gallons of the real thing.

The land in this region is very demanding both on men and on the vineyards, and the climate is not too generous either. Winters are often very harsh, and while the summer heat speeds up the ripening process, during the spring temperatures often stay below the 32° F mark until around May. Winegrowers try to outsmart the weather using home-made techniques to protect the vines from the frost. These range from placing small heaters at the base of the vines to sprinkling water which then freezes around the grape buds and creates an insulating coating of ice that protects them from low temperatures.

The only grape variety growing in this area is chardonnay, locally known as *beaunois*.

The *appellation* comprises four ranks of wine, each with very different characteristics.

Chablis *Grands Crus* differ from their companions first of all by their golden yellow color. They drink well up to eight years following harvest and some vintage wines can be kept for ten years and still improve. These wines, the most remarkable of the region, all come from a 217- to 220-acre vineyard area situated on the right bank of the Serein river and broken up into the plots (or *climats*) of Blanchots, Bougros, les Clos, Grenouilles, Preuses, Valmur and Vaudésir.

The Chablis *Premiers Crus* have a pale golden color, with an occasional green tint. Under good storage conditions, they can keep for up to six years. Younger *Grands Crus* are produced in twenty-seven *climats*, covering 1100 to 1480 acres.

Chablis vineyards take up more than half of the whole *appellation* area, stretching over 3700 acres and scattered among 19 districts.

These white wines are very dry, with a clear color, lively and fresh. They are best drunk within the first three years of harvesting.

Finally, Petit Chablis are very fruity *primeurs* (young wines), to be consumed within the first year. The vineyards are often located on clay soil and production is fairly small.

WHICH CHEESE?

MONT D'OR
CROTTIN DE CHAVIGNOL
POULIGNY-SAINT-PIERRE
CHAOURCE

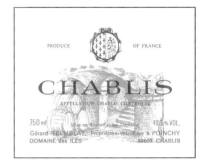

CHARACTERISTICS

Chablis premiers crus *are light, nervy, with a tang of almond.*
After three years, they become perfectly rich and lively.

25

CÔTE DE NUITS

GRAPE VARIETIES

FOR WHITE WINES
CHARDONNAY
PINOT BLANC

FOR RED WINES
PINOT NOIR
GAMAY NOIR

Above, *Clos Vougeot.*

MARSANNAY-LA-CÔTE

Marsannay-la-Côte lacks *Grands* and *Premiers Crus*, but still has its own distinctive features. It makes some rosé wines under the *appellation* Burgundy-Clairet or Rosé de Marsannay. It is a fruity and well-balanced wine, reputed to be one of the best in France.

FIXIN

Fixin, famous for its two-color painted rooftops, has 500 acres of *appellation* vineyards, a tenth of which is devoted to five *Premiers Crus*, which are sturdy and long-lived.

GEVREY-CHAMBERTIN

This 1100-acre *appellation* vineyard is one of the most fertile of the district.
The two dominant wines are the

great Chambertin and Chambertin-Clos-de-Bèze.

MOREY-SAINT-DENIS

This communal *appellation* covers 270 acres outside *Grands Crus* vineyards.
Clos-Saint-Denis raises one of the lightest reds of the Côte de Nuits. Less sturdy and robust than its companions in Clos de Tart and Roche, it stands out for its superb color and delicate aromas.

CHAMBOLLE-MUSIGNY

When you hear of a vineyard charmingly spread over 315 acres, you know they are talking about the Chambolle-Musigny *appellation*.
The local *Grands Crus* are Bonnes-Mares and the fabulous Musigny, which enjoys a worldwide reputation.

FLAGEY-ÉCHEZEAUX

Flagey-Échezeaux, halfway between Vougeot and Vosne-Romanée, includes three *Premiers Crus* and two *Grands Crus*, Grands-Échezeaux and Échezeaux.

NUITS-SAINT-GEORGES

Quite surprisingly, Nuits-Saint-Georges does not have any *Grands Crus*. The wines take a long time to reach maturity and age very well. The communal vineyard covers about 740 acres and includes at least twenty-nine *Premiers Crus*.

VOUGEOT

Vougeot is not only famous for its vineyards; Clos de Vougeot is a major landmark of the national heritage. However, its tiny *appellation* of less than 42 acres is well worth a mention.

Four *Premiers Crus* take up half of this limited vineyard area. Clos Vougeot enjoys such a widespread reputation that its prestigious name represents France all over the world. These wines have in common a good structure, opulence, a spicy character and a long impact on the palate. They are quite robust and colored, with a powerful and extremely refined nose.

VOSNE-ROMANÉE

This small *appellation* of just over 495 acres includes as many as thirteen *Premiers Crus* and some of Burgundy's finest wines. It has been one of the most jealously kept and sought-after vineyards of France for centuries and it is considered so precious that its extension is calculated to the square yard.

The Romanée-Conti legendary vineyard is humbly marked by an engraved stone half concealed in a wall.

The adjoining Romanée-Saint-Vivant estate distinguishes itself from its neighbor by one crucial word: perfection.

WHICH CHEESE?

ÉPOISSES
BRIE
PONT-L'ÉVÈQUE
CAMEMBERT
NEUFCHÂTEL
MAROILLES

Above, the village of Nuits-Saint-Georges.

CHARACTERISTICS

Côte de Nuits wines are firm and very colored reds. They are full bodied and harmonious on the palate. Some Côte de Nuits, like Chambolle-Musigny, are exceptionally delicate, displaying subtle aromas of red fruit.

27

CÔTE DE BEAUNE

GRAPE VARIETIES

FOR WHITE WINES
CHARDONNAY

FOR RED WINES
PINOT NOIR
PINOT LIEBAULT
PINOT BEUROT

Above, Clos Chevaliers-Montrachet.

Below, the Jaffelin cellars at Beaune.

CORTON

Corton stretches over 220 acres, divided among estates whose names may be hyphenated to Corton on the labels.

At the top of the hillsides, where the soil has a high concentration of limestone, chardonnay grapes achieve wonders. Corton-Charlemagne is a golden colored wine, ranked among the greatest whites of the world.

ALOXE-CORTON

This *appellation*, extending over 287 acres incorporates some plots of Ladoix-Serrigny and Pernand-Vergelesses, while the rest covers eight *Premiers Crus*. The main ones are: Les Chaillots, Les Meix, Basses-Mourettes. They have in common a cherry taste and woody aromas.

PERNAND-VERGELESSES

The communal A.O.C. Pernand-Vergelesses covers over 287 acres, half of which is devoted to five *Premiers Crus*.

SAVIGNY-LÈS-BEAUNE

Savigny reds, which are the main of twenty-two *Premiers Crus*, are Vergelesses, Marconnets, Dominode, Lavières, Serpentières, Peuillets and Aux Guettes.

BEAUNE

Like a real wine capital, Beaune harvests its own wines.

Among its forty-two *Premiers Crus*, the most remarkable are: Les Grèves, Clos des Mouches, Les Fèves, Les Bressandes, Les Marconnets, Aux Cras and Champimonts. The Beaune A.O.C. area is included in the Côte de Beaune *appellation*.

POMMARD

Pommard boasts an 833-acre vineyard (310 of which are *Premiers Crus*) almost entirely planted with pinot noir grapes.

At the top of the list of twenty-eight *Premiers Crus* is Les Chaponnières. Grands-Épenots and Petits-Épenots, Rugiens-Bas and Rugiens-Hauts also deserve mention.

VOLNAY

Volnay stretches on 526 acres of land, half of which is devoted to thirty-four *Premiers Crus*. After Les Caillerets, undisputed top of the rank, it is also worth naming Les Aussy, Carelles Dessus, La Gigotte, Lassolle, Les Lurets, Piture Dessus, Robardelle, Ronceret, Taillepieds and Clos du Verseuil.

MONTHÉLIE

This village is blessed with eleven *Premiers Crus*. The best ones are: Champs-Fulliot, Cas-Rougeot, La Taupine, Le Clos Gauthey, Le Château-Gaillard, Le Meix-Bataille, Les Riottes.

AUXEY-DURESSES

This *appellation* includes nine *Premiers Crus*, covering one fourth of the communal vineyard area. Among them, Les Duresses, Clos-du-Val, Les Breterins, Les Bas-des-Duresses.

MEURSAULT

At Meursault, chardonnay and pinot noir grapes are trained on a soil made of magnesium- and iron-rich limestone. When they ripen, they reach the peak of excellence. The *appellation* covers 1060 acres divided among Meursault, Blagny and Volnay. It comprises about twenty *Premiers Crus*, of which Les Perrières and Clos des Perrières are the most remarkable.

PULIGNY-MONTRACHET
CHASSAGNE-MONTRACHET

The hostile soil of Puligny-Montrachet and Chassagne-Montrachet is a blessing for chardonnay grapes. This is the home of France's best dry white wines. The *Grands Crus* are Montrachet and Bâtard-Montrachet (Puligny and Chassagne), Chevalier-Montrachet, Bienvenue-Bâtard-Montrachet (Puligny), Criots-Bâtard-Montrachet (Chassagne). Chassagne-Montrachet makes both red and white wines. Morgeot, Grandes Ruchottes and Cailleret feature among the best growths.

SANTENAY

The Santenay *appellation* includes twelve *Premiers Crus*, such as Gravières, Clos de Tavannes, La Comme, Beauregard. La Maladière and Clos Rousseau deserve a special mention.

WHICH CHEESE?

REBLOCHON
CHABICHOU
CROTTIN DE CHAVIGNOL
PONT-L'ÉVÊQUE
ÉPOISSES

CHARACTERISTICS

Red wines are racy, generous, solid, vigorous, with perfect tannic levels. They have a full body and aroma and are made for the long term. The white wines are perfumed and lively.

29

CÔTE CHALONNAISE

GRAPE VARIETIES

ALIGOTÉ
CHARDONNAY
GAMAY
PINOR GRIS
PINOT NOIR

CÔTE CHALONNAISE

This is the natural extension of the Beaune region. Here too, vineyards are trained with pinot noir and chardonnay, which in Givry is combined with pinot blanc. Winemaking methods are the same as in

Above, The Mercurey vineyard.

the adjoining region, but the quality of the soil is poorer. In spite of the excellence of some growths,

they lack the panache of their illustrious neighbors. Bouzeron prides itself of being a unique village. Here, they make Bourgogne Aligoté Bouzeron, the finest of Burgundy's aligoté wines, which enjoys a specific *appellation*.

MERCUREY

Every year, this *appellation* produces about three thousand bottles of the distinguished white Mercurey.
The best Mercurey wines are *Premiers Crus*: Clos du Roi, Les Voyens, Clos Marcilly, Clos des Fourneaux and Clos des Montaigus.

MONTAGNY

This vineyard covers Montagny-lès-Buxy, Buxy, Saint-Vallerin and Jully-lès-Buxy and comprises about sixty *Premiers Crus*. Beside the communal *appellation*, there is also a sub-regional A.O.C., Bourgogne Côte Chalonnaise, which covers some vineyards divided among about forty districts in the areas of Chagny, Givry and Buxy.

MÂCONNAIS

This vineyard covers a swathe of land which is about 9.3 miles wide and over 30 miles long, stretching west of the river Saône.
This vast territory has different types of soil, with different combi-

nations of limestone, clay, chalk, slate, silica and sand. The Mâcon-Villages *appellation* concerns forty-three districts of the Mâcon area and is of excellent value. Other sub-regional *appellations* are Mâcon (or Pinot-Chardonnay-Mâcon for white wines) and Mâcon Supérieur. The whites, made from chardonnay and pinot blanc, are supple and fruity.

SAINT-VÉRAN

On the border between the Chalons hillsides and the Beaujolais region, Saint-Véran is produced by the vineyards of Saint-Vérand, Chânes, Chasselas, Solutré, Davayé, Prissé, Leynes and Saint-Amour-Bellevue. This is quite a new *appellation*, created as recently as 1971. It indicates a dry white wine made from chardonnay.

POUILLY-FUISSÉ

Only four districts enjoy this extraordinary *appellation*, which extends over 1700 acres of vineyards facing east-south-east. They are Vergisson, Solutré, Fuissé and Chaintré.

POUILLY-LOCHÉ
POUILLY-VINZELLES

Pouilly-Loché and Pouilly-Vinzelles are neighboring *appellations* of Fuissé. They produce similar wines which, however, have their own sufficiently distinctive personalities. Pouilly-Vinzelles develops a bouquet of floral smells of acacia and peony with a hint of honey.

WHICH CHEESE?

COMTÉ
CANTAL
SELLES-SUR-CHER
POULIGNY-SAINT-PIERRE
BRIE

CHARACTERISTICS

Mercurey wines have a lively taste and a floral nose, with delicate aromas.
Mâcon white and red wines have good color and combine elegance with a complex bouquet.
Pouilly-Fuissé develops a harmonious variety of fruity aromas with a honey finish.

31

BEAUJOLAIS

GRAPE VARIETIES

GAMAY NOIR

SAINT-AMOUR

At Saint-Amour-Bellevue, the limestone soil of the Mâcon area is replaced by the characteristic granite terrains of the higher Beaujolais district, which here are mixed with schist and sandstone. The well reputed Saint-Amour is one of the most pleasant Beaujolais growths.

Above, a Beaujolais vineyard.

JULIÉNAS

Juliénas comes from the districts of Juliénas, Jullié, Émeringes and Pruzilly, where gamay grows on a granite- and clay-rich soil and pro-

duces a firm, fruity and robust purple-colored wine. Juliénas is one of the Beaujolais growths which ages best; some vintages can easily withstand five to six years of aging.

CHÉNAS

The mix of granite and manganese greatly favors both the gamay grapes and the oak trees that used to abound here and gave the name to this region. This *appellation* covers the plots of Chénas and La-Chapelle-de-Guinchay.

MOULIN-À-VENT

Gamay develops all its potential in this wine, defined by its devotees as having the grace of a Beaujolais and the prestige of a Burgundy. Moulin-à-Vent wines are made in Chénas and Romanèche-Thorins.

FLEURIE

Fleurie is best drunk after two years, embellished with all the charm of youth.

CHIROUBLES

Here, gamay produces a brilliant red wine, light to the point of airiness. It is tender, lively, elegant and merry.

MORGON

This vineyard dates back to the 10th century.
Here, gamay produces a wine defined as Burgundy because of its re-

semblance with the great reds made in the Côte d'Or. It is more robust than other Beaujolais growths and needs time to develop fully.

RÉGNIÉ

This *appellation* was admitted to the highest ranks of the Beaujolais classification in 1988.
Régnié hosts Grange Charton, property of the Hospices of Beaujeu, which were founded in 1240 and play the same role in this region as the Hospices de Beaune in Burgundy.

BROUILLY-CÔTES-DE-BROUILLY

Here, the vineyards flank the hill, pushing up near the top. They benefit from a soil containing granite and greenish-blue schist.
They cover an area of about 3700 acres. Four fifths of the land produce Brouilly, while the core of the vineyards on the slopes of the mountain are devoted to Côtes-de-Brouilly. These wines are concentrated and have a deep purple color. They contain more alcohol than the other Beaujolais growths.

BEAUJOLAIS-VILLAGES

The districts producing the best wines enjoy the Beaujolais-Villages *appellation*.
In 1956, the wine-growers of the northern part of Beaujolais launched Beaujolais Nouveau on the market. Year after year, the popularity of this wine increased dramatically. At the same time, the production area was extended to cover the whole of the Beaujolais region.

WHICH CHEESE?

MUNSTER
FOURME
LAGUIOLE
BRIE DE MEAUX
LIVAROT

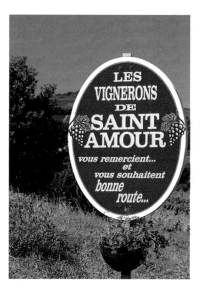

CHARACTERISTICS

Beaujolais wines have a pretty, brilliant red color, a fruity nose and a fine and assertive taste. Their perfumes are complex and evoke exotic fruit with a touch of red fruit and peach. They also possess a distinctive long-lasting aroma, that is enhanced with aging.

33

CÔTES DU RHÔNE

This appellation *covers a vast territory. It starts south of Lyon, then stretches along the Rhône valley, which is a thin strip of land caught between the river and the mountainous ridge of the Massif Central. It then slowly grows larger, touching the Drôme valley, disappears for a moment and finally spreads out, embracing every little rise, every small valley and climbing up to the foothills of the Alps. The Durance district stops this expansion and sets the borders with the wine-growing region of Provence.*

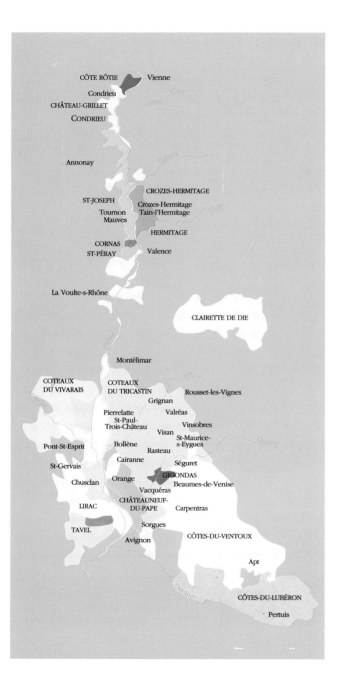

The appellation *Côtes du Rhône is divided into* two very distinct zones.

NORTHERN CÔTES DU RHÔNE

This region often uses only one grape variety, syrah, for the reds and viognier, roussanne and marsanne for the whites. This results in very small appellations like Château-Grillet (7.4 acres) or considerably larger ones like Crozes Hermitage (over 2500 acres).

SOUTHERN CÔTES DU RHÔNE

This area is extremely diverse, giving rise to about twenty different vine varieties. It is the great region where Côtes du Rhône, Côtes du Rhône-Villages, Côtes du Tricastin, Ventoux and Lubéron are produced.

THE REGIONAL APPELLATIONS

Côtes du Rhône: these wines are produced over the whole regional appellation *and are made mainly from syrah in the northern part and from the twenty-three varieties permitted for the northern Côtes du Rhône appellation. They range from 11 to 13 percent alcohol.*
Côtes du Rhône-Villages: This appellation *was created in 1966 and covers 48 districts, 26 of which are allowed to append their names to the more generic 'Villages' appellation, for a total of 17 communal appellations.*
They contain a minimum of 12 percent alcohol for rosé and white wines and 12.5 percent for the reds. The mix of vine varieties and yield regulations are stricter than those applying to the Côtes du Rhône primeur or new wine. These wines are released on 15th November and follow the same principle of rapid vinification as the Beaujolais, which makes them fresh and very aromatic drinks.

CÔTES DU RHÔNE

GRAPE VARIETIES

FOR RED WINES
SYRAH

FOR WHITE WINES
VIOGNIER
ROUSSANNE
MARSANNE

CÔTE RÔTIE

Vineyards cling on such steep slopes that terraces were created, supported by stone walls. This area is divided into Côte Blonde and Côte Brune, depending on the quality of the soil. The first has a marly, chalky soil which produces wines that are supple and dynamic in their youth. The other has a soil containing more clay, with a touch of iron oxide, which makes more robust and long-lived wines. The production of this 345-acre vineyard is around 160 000 gallons.

CONDRIEU

This *Appellation d'Origine Con-trôlée* was created in 1940. Its vineyards grow on an area of 100 acres, nicknamed the 'darling hillsides'. The region produces a very perfumed white wine with a taste markedly influenced by environmental factors. Condrieu is harvested late, and when it is bottled after the winter, it makes a mellow product. If, instead, it is kept in barrels for about a year and a half, the fermentation process continues, giving a 'dry' wine, which is sweet, racy and with bouquet and which, once it reaches maturity, develops fruity

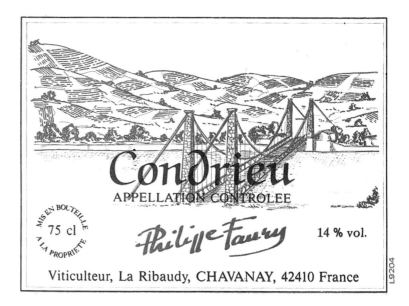

Condrieu
APPELLATION CONTROLEE

MIS EN BOUTEILLE
A LA PROPRIETE
75 cl

Philippe Faury

14 % vol.

Viticulteur, La Ribaudy, CHAVANAY, 42410 France

L9204

aromas. Production is not large, remaining below 53 000 gallons.

HERMITAGE

This growth is named after a lord who then became a hermit. Syrah is the dominating variety and may be blended with a maximum of 15 percent of the white varieties of roussanne and marsanne. Other famous estates are Méal, Rocoule, Beaume and Maison-Blanche.

CROZES-HERMITAGE

This *appellation*, created in 1937, benefits from the excellent reputation of its distinguished neighbor. Since 1952, it has experienced a considerable expansion and now covers around 2500 acres, spread over the districts of Serves, Érôme, Gervans, Larnage, Crozes-Hermitage, Mercurol, Chanos-Curson, Beaumont-Monteux, La Roche-de-Glun, Pont de l'Isère. The overall production reaches 1.3 million gallons, a tenth of which consists of white wines.

SAINT-JOSEPH

Stretching along the right bank of the Rhône valley, from the Loire region down to a few miles from the town of Valence, this *appellation* - established in 1956 - covers 12 500 acres and twenty-two districts of the Ardèche region. Microclimates play an important role in local production.
These vineyards extend from the village of Limony and follow the left bank of the Rhône, from Tournon down to Châteaubourg.

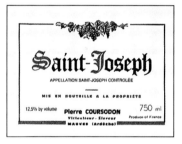

CHARACTERISTICS

Hermitage has a deep red color; it is a wine with great class and a strong impact on the palate, developing its roundness on a sturdy structure.
In their best vintages, both whites and reds can easily withstand twenty years of aging.
Saint-Joseph wines have an elegant allure and are well-balanced on the palate.

CÔTES DU RHÔNE

GRAPE VARIETIES

FOR RED WINES
SYRAH

FOR WHITE WINES
VIOGNIER
ROUSSANNE
MARSANNE

CORNAS

Cornas is a small 185-acre vineyard producing around 79 000 gallons every year. It obtained its *appellation* status in 1938. This wine has a very dark color and was highly appreciated by Charlemagne. Later, Louis XV described it as a 'beautiful black wine'. It is made from syrah grapes.

SAINT-PÉRAY

This small *appellation*, covering only about 125 acres, was created in 1936. It produces dry white wines from roussanne and marsanne grapes on marly-limestone soil. Bottle fermentation has been the practice here for about a century now, giving excellent Saint-Péray sparkling wines.

RASTEAU

At the heart of the Vaucluse region, this *appellation* - dating back to 1944 - covers less than 500 acres, including the alluvial terraces of Aigues and Ouvèze and the red clay terrace of Rasteau, rich in pebbles of quartz and limestone.

BEAUMES-DE-VENISE

The same principle applies to the region of Beaume, which fifteen years ago resumed the production of fortified wines known as *vins doux naturels* and the more spirit dominated *vins de liqueur*. They are made from the muscat variety called *à petits grains* (small-berried) or from muscat of Frontignan. This region also makes Côtes du Rhône wines followed by the suffix Beaumes-de-Venise. They are served in a special bottle called 'venetian', specially designed for these drinks.

VACQUEYRAS

This new *appellation*, created in 1990, is dominated by the grenache variety, which accounts for at least half the blend of these generous red wines. The rest is usually syrah and mourvèdre, completed by other local varieties. Production is around 740 000 gallons a year.

SÉGURET

The medieval village of Séguret is surrounded by a vineyard extending over 2000 acres.
There is an old wine-making tradition here which probably dates back to Roman times. Classified as one of the prettiest villages of France, Séguret has kept its medieval charm.

CAIRANNE

Vineyards started developing on the pretty slopes of Cairanne hillsides under the influence of soldier monks. Nowadays, winegrowers still make very vigorous and tannic wines, which usually require some aging.

CHÂTEAUNEUF-DU-PAPE

This vineyard stretches for 7500

acres between Orange and Avignon, over the districts of Orange, Sorgues-Bédarrides and Châteauneuf-du-Pape. The terrain is alluvial, made of red clay, with pebbles washed up by the Rhône in the Quaternary. These pebbles retain the daytime heat and release it during the night. The rich variety of grapes allows every wine-grower to adapt their assembly of blends to the environmental conditions of individual zones. Grenache, which used to be the dominant variety, has now been outweighed by richer grapes such as syrah, mourvèdre and muscadin. Production reaches 2.6 million gallons, 90 percent of which is red wine.

TAVEL

Tavel vineyards grow on the right bank of the river Rhône, a few miles away from Châteauneuf-du-Pape and Avignon. They cover an area of 2000 acres and produce over 1 million gallons of wine. Grenache is the dominant grape, which can constitute up to 60 percent of the blend. Other main varieties are cinsault (minimum of 15 percent of the blend), syrah (which gives the color of the wine) and mourvèdre (which gives it more body).

WHICH CHEESE?

BROCCIO DE CORSE
BLEU DES CAUSSES
BLEU D'AUVERGNE
BLEU DE GEX
ÉPOISSES

Opposite, the vineyard and village of Séguret.

CHARACTERISTICS

Châteauneuf-du-Pape used to need several years aging to reach maturity. Modern wine-making techniques can produce a wine that matures after four to five years.

CÔTES DU RHÔNE

GRAPE VARIETIES
FOR RED WINES
SYRAH
GRENACHE
CINSAULT
CARIGNAN
MOURVÈDRE
FOR WHITE WINES
VIOGNIER
ROUSSANNE
MARSANNE
MUSCAT
UGNI BLANC
CLAIRETTE

GIGONDAS

This vineyard produces about 1 million gallons of red wine and a small quantity of rosé, mainly made from black grenache (65 percent), syrah, mourvèdre and cinsault (25 percent). The blend is completed by Côtes du Rhône varieties.

LIRAC

This *appellation*, established in 1947, covers the arid and pebbly hillsides north of Tavel. It also includes the districts of Saint-Laurent-des-Arbres, Saint-Géniès-de-Comolas and Roquemaure.

CÔTES DU RHÔNE

The Côtes du Rhône *appellation*, granted in 1937, covers 98 800 acres, including 163 districts spread over six regions: Ardèche, Drôme, Gard, Loire, Rhône and Vaucluse. Twenty-three different grape varieties are used. The main ones are: syrah, clairette, cinsault, mourvèdre, roussette, picpoul, roussanne, marsanne, terret noir, picardan, viognier, bourboulenc and others. Although it is possible to blend wines made in the northern and southern zones, the latter is by far the bigger producer of simple Côtes du Rhône.

CÔTES DU VIVARAIS

The Côtes du Vivarais vineyards were granted VDQS (superior quality) status in 1962. They grow on the limestone soil of the Ardèche plateau, on the right bank of the river Rhône. The land is planted with the typical varieties of the Côtes du Rhône region (grenache, cinsault, mourvèdre, picpoul, syrah, bourboulenc, clairette, ugni blanc,...)
Only the accessory grapes aubun and carignan are not allowed to constitute more than 40 percent of the blend.

COTEAUX DU TRICASTIN

The hills of Tricastin stretch over more than 5000 acres south of Montélimar. They were classified VDQS in 1964 and were subsequently promoted to full A.O.C. status in 1973.
The traditional vine varieties of the Côtes du Rhône grow here on a red-clay soil, mixed with limestone and gravel and produce fine and fruity reds. White wines, made in much smaller amounts, are dry and pleasantly perfumed.

CLAIRETTE DE DIE

The black and heavy soil made from Jurassic marl is particularly suitable for muscat vines. They are combined with the clairette variety, which adds lightness and freshness to the final product. Fizzy wine can be made in two ways. The first is the *champenoise* - or bottle fermentation - method, with the addition of bottling liquor. Alternatively, the local traditional method called *dioise* is adopted. Fermentation is started by the natural grape sugar and the second fermentation lasts four months. This gives a more marked taste of muscat. This kind of clairette is signalled on the label by the word 'tradition'.

CÔTES DU VENTOUX

The *appellation* zone of about 17 000 acres produces wines whose quality has improved considerably. This was reflected in 1973 by their promotion from VDQS to full A.O.C. status.
Red wines can be tannic and sturdy when vineyards are well exposed to the sun.

CÔTES DE LUBERON

This area, classified VDQS in 1951, was finally recognised as A.O.C. in 1988.
The dominant grape varieties for the reds are grenache, syrah (which together must not exceed 50 percent), cinsault and carignan. White wines may incorporate ugni blanc (less than 80 percent), grenache blanc, clairette, bourboulenc and vermentino.

WHICH CHEESE?

SAINT-NECTAIRE
FOURME

CHARACTERISTICS

Côtes-du-Rhône-Villages reds made in the Drôme region are very fruity and should be drunk young.
The ones produced in the Vaucluse taste of pepper and liquorice and can keep for two to three years, depending on their vineyard of origin and the amount of syrah in the blend.

41

PROVENCE-CÔTE D'AZUR

FOR RED WINES
MOURVÈDRE
CINSAULT
CARIGNAN
GRENACHE

FOR WHITE WINES
UGNI BLANC
CLAIRETTE
SÉMILLON

Provence's wine-growing region covers 12 350 acres and comprises six Appellations d'Origine Contrôlées.

CASSIS

Cassis produces about 158 000 gallons of wine, two thirds of which are a renowned white.

BANDOL

These are original red wines, aging 18 months in barrels.

BELLET

Bellet's wine production is rather modest, in the region of 20 000 gallons.

PALETTE

This tiny 47.5-acre vineyard mainly makes powerful reds.

CÔTES DE PROVENCE

This region is dominated by rosés (60 percent) and red wines (35 percent).

COTEAUX D'AIX-EN-PROVENCE

Vineyards can be found around Aix and on the superb site of Baux-de-Provence.

Provence makes red as well as white and rosé wines. However, its fame mostly comes from the production of rosés, reputed to be among the best in France.

CÔTES DE PROVENCE

Production is divided into three main sectors: the coast, stretching from La Ciotat to Saint-Tropez (excluding the Bandol region), a part of the Maures mountains, namely in the valley of the river Arc and the valley of the Argens. The variety of environments and the many microclimates - some more humid and more windy than others - make this *appellation* an extremely rich one.

The region is dominated by the rosé wines, which account for nearly two thirds of total production. They are very varied, encompassing virtually all hues of pink and with very different tastes.

PALETTE

This is the rarest wine of the whole of Provence (5200 gallons per year). It is made in a tiny 30-acre vineyard growing on a limestone outcrop between Tholonet and Meyreuil and a few miles south of Aix-en-Provence.

There are only two estates sharing this *appellation*: Château Simone, on the left bank of the river Arc is the main one. Palette was awarded its A.O.C. status in 1948. As many as twenty-five grape varieties are allowed.

COTEAUX D'AIX-EN-PROVENCE

The Coteaux d'Aix-en-Provence *appellation* encompasses about 7400 acres all around the town of

that name. It is an area sheltered from the mistral wind and with an ideal climate for wine-growing. It borders the Durance valley to the north and the Rhône to the west. It also includes land around the Berre lagoon, stretches along the foot of the Sainte-Victoire mountain and ends to the east in a thin strip of land into the Var region, at the border with Artigues.

One of the most remarkable growths is Château Vignelaure.

WHICH CHEESE?

PICODON
BROCCIO DE CORSE

CHARACTERISTICS

All colors of Palette wines produced at Château Simone are very fine and elegant.
The reds are suave and warm and they age well; the rosés are arguably among the best on the market at the moment.
The whites, too, are of high quality for southern standards.

43

PROVENCE-CÔTE D'AZUR

CASSIS

This vineyard zone of 385 acres grows on limestone hills all around the port of Cassis, on the slopes furrowed by creeks near Marseilles. This wine was accredited A.O.C. in 1936, but wine-making dates back to the early centuries of our era. The region also makes reds and dry rosés quite similar to those of Bandol, with a minimum of 11 percent alcohol.

BANDOL

Seven districts are included in this *appellation*: Bandol, La Cadière

On the right, a Provence vineyard.

d'Azur, le Castellet, Ollioules, Évenos, Saint-Cyr-sur-Mer and Beausol. Bandol wines must have at least 11 percent alcohol.

BELLET

This tiny *appellation* growing on a gravely , silica-rich terrain stands in the middle of the flower-growing hinterland of Nice. Bellet wines were gradually disappearing when, about ten years ago, they were launched again by a dynamic owner.

CORSICA

In Corsica there is a real passion for wine. Since ancient times, vines have been grown on the steep slopes of its mountains and on the flanks of its sunny valleys. In April 1976, the Corsican wine *appellation* 'Vins de Corse' was re-organised and awarded to about sixty districts. The regions of

Côteaux du Cap Corse, Porto-Vecchio, Figari, Sartène, Ajaccio, Calvi and Patrimonio may add their names to the generic *appellation*. A.O.C. wines account for around 20 percent of the island's production, the *vins de pays appellation* for 30 percent and the table wine *appellation vins de table* for the rest.

WHICH CHEESE?

DRY GOAT CHEESES
PICODON
BROCCIO DE CORSE

THE CORSICAN APPELLATIONS

Corsican wines are grouped into eight A.O.C., of which six are 'Vins de Corse'.

VINS DE CORSE

These wines are produced throughout the island, with the exception of the region of Patrimonio. There are five local appellations, that bear the name 'Vins de Corse' followed by the district or region: Coteaux du Cap Corse, Calvi, Sartène, Figari, Porto-Vecchio.

CHARACTERISTICS

White Cassis made from ugni blanc enjoys a better reputation than its red counterpart. It is a dry and not very acid wine. Bandol rosés are supple and fruity and are produced from the same grape varieties as the reds. They are mainly drunk locally, to accompany traditional regional dishes.

45

LANGUEDOC-ROUSSILLON

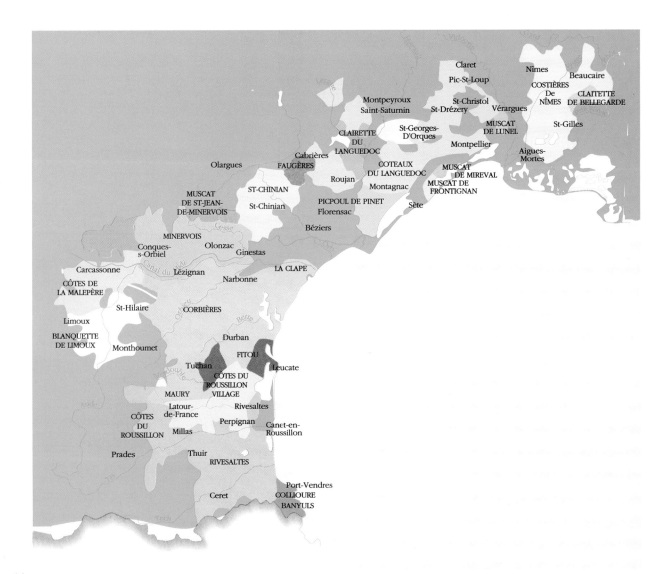

This very large vineyard area, comprising the regions of Gard, Hérault and Aude, was started by the Greeks in the Agde region in the 4th century B.C.

In the late 'seventies, local wine-growers generated a real revolution by planting new combinations of vine varieties and introducing new methods of vinification.

COSTIÈRES DE NÎMES

This *appellation*, known as Costières du Gard until 1986, is mainly gathered around the town of Nîmes. Out of a total of 69 000 acres, only about 10 000 acres qualify for the production of *appellation* wine.

COTEAUX DU LANGUEDOC

This regional *appellation* is actually made up of about ten different wine-growing areas, including 120 districts, mostly in the Hérault region. Only 39 500 acres of this immense territory of 123 500 acres are *appellation* vineyards.

LES CORBIÈRES

From the south-west of Carcassonne to the Mediterranean sea, vine-growing takes up 103 700 acres of arid mountain terrain and sunny coastal areas swept by the mistral and the Cers. A total of 61 800 acres produce *appellation* wine.

SAINT-CHINIAN – FAUGÈRES

These two *appellations*, created in 1982, are part of the large family of Coteaux du Languedoc wines. They cover the very gravely and schist-rich slopes north-west of Hérault, on the high areas of Saint-Chinian and Faugères.

FITOU

This 5 000-acre vineyard zone south of Narbonne includes the best districts of Corbières: the Hautes Corbières at the foot of mount Tauch, near Tuchan, and the coastal Corbières Maritimes, overhanging the Mediterranean sea and the Leucate lagoon, which overlooks the village of Fitou. Almost all wine-growers belong to one of the seven local co-operatives, which produce about 2.6 gallons of red wines.

Above, the hilly vineyard of Corbières.

Below, the Cucugnan vineyard.

Below, the Corbières vineyard.

LANGUEDOC-ROUSSILLON

GRAPE VARIETIES

FOR RED WINES
SYRAH
MOURVÈDRE
PICPOUL
LLADONER PELUT
GRENACHE
TERRET

FOR WHITE WINES
MAUZAC
CLAIRETTE
CINSAULT
MACCABÉO
MUSCAT

CUVÉE TRIANON
1990
CHATEAU
VILLERAMBERT JULIEN
MINERVOIS
APPELLATION CONTROLÉE
MIS EN BOUTEILLE AU CHATEAU
Produce of France
750 ml   Marcel Julien, 11160 Caunes Minervois   12% alc. vol.

CHARACTERISTICS

The making of Banyuls, the most famous of Roussillon wines, has to comply with regulations concerning short pruning, no irrigation, mutage before 31 December and at least 15 percent alcohol.
Banyuls Grand Cru undergoes an initial aging process in the open; maturation is then completed in wooden casks.

MINERVOIS

The Minervois A.O.C., in the region of Aude but also encroaching on Hérault, groups about sixty districts over 9800 acres at the foot of the Montagne Noire, in the north of the Corbières region. The combination of vine varieties is extremely rich.

BLANQUETTE DE LIMOUX

In Limoux, they have been making sparkling white wine from blanquette grapes (a local name for mauzac) for over four centuries now. The wine sparkles naturally after a second fermentation in the bottle, exploiting the inherent grape sugar remaining after the first fermentation. This method helps to keep the fruity apple character of the mauzac grape.

ROUSSILLON

Lying on the administrative border of the eastern Pyrenees, Roussillon is the producer *par excellence* of *vins doux naturels*. The soil is so harsh that vines look as though they have been pulled up from schist. Yet its lights, perfumes and warmth can be found in the wines of Collioure, Banyuls and Rivesaltes.

RIVESALTES

The vineyard of *vins doux naturels* covers 74 000 acres in Roussillon, comprising 115 districts of the eastern Pyrenees and the Aude. North of Perpignan, 44 500 acres of red soil are devoted exclusively to Rivesaltes. It is one of France's smallest yields (15 tons per acre). Rivesaltes - which means high coasts in Catalan - produces two kinds of sweet wine.

RIVESALTES MUSCAT

This superb amber-colored wine is made exclusively from muscat blanc à petit grains and muscat of Alexandria. Its 11 100-acre vineyards are scattered among all the districts of Rivesaltes, Banyuls and Maury *appellations*.

RIVESALTES *APPELLATION*

It includes red, white or rosé wines. Reds are obtained by macerating the must with the pulp during fermentation.
Whites and rosés, on the other hand, are fermented separately from the pulp. It is worth mentioning the famous Rivesaltes Rancio, which acquires a rancio taste after lengthy aging in barrels exposed to the sun.

BANYULS

This *appellation* covers four districts: Collioure, Port-Vendres, Cerbère and Banyuls. Its distinctive taste derives from grenache, the dominant grape variety, which accounts for at least 50 percent of the blend. The best Banyuls are arguably the Banyuls *Grands Crus*, which have a higher proportion of grenache and even stricter wine-making procedures (destemming and maceration for at least five days before chemical sterilisation and compulsory wood aging for at least three years).

CÔTES DU ROUSSILLON

It is France's southernmost A.O.C. and was created in 1977.

It stretches over a large area south of the Corbières region down to the Albères mountains and the Spanish border.

However, the best parts are located along the Agly river valley, north of Perpignan and on the arid plateau at the foot of the Canigou mountains and of the Ferrouillèdes and the Corbières foothills.

The soil is a real geological melting pot. Here, one can find virtually everything: red clay, granite, schist, mixtures of clay and limestone. On this soil, about ten different varieties are cultivated: carignan, limoult, grenache, lladoner pelut, improved by mourvèdre, syrah and maccabéo for whites. Twenty-five districts spread over an area of about 6200 acres have the right to the Côtes-du-Roussillon-Villages *appellation*. Only two of them, though, have been granted the privilege to append their name to the *appellation* on the label: Caramany and Latour-de-France. These districts are only allowed vinification by carbonic maceration.

WHICH CHEESE?

ROQUEFORT
FOURME
BLUE CHEESES

LANGUEDOC

The Coteaux du Languedoc ap-pellation covers thirty-four districts and twelve zones. Some produce A.O.C. wines such as Fi-tau, Faugères, Saint Chinian, Muscat de Lunel wines, Mireval and Frontignan; others bear the V.D.Q.S. label, like Corbrières, Minervois, Picpoul, Costières-du-Gard.

ROUSSILLON

Eight appellations share the west-ern Pyrenees region: Côtes du Roussillon, Côtes du Roussillon-Villages, Collioure, Rivesaltes, Muscat de Rivesaltes, Maury, Banyuls and Banyuls Grand Cru.

RANCIO

A few natural sweet wines aged in oak barrels are entitled to be called 'Rancio'. They have a love-ly golden color and very delicate aroma.

THE SOUTH WEST

Above, harvesting.

BERGERAC

This town has not always been on very good terms with its impressive neighbor Bordeaux, and yet both combinations of vine varieties and wine-making techniques are strikingly similar.

The Côtes de Bergerac *appellation* covers a smaller area. Red wines must contain between 11 and 13 percent alcohol, while for the sweet whites it may vary from 12 to 15 percent.

The reds are considerably more robust than their simple *appellation* counterparts. They have a dark color and are suited for aging.

PÉCHARMANT

The origin of this A.O.C., created

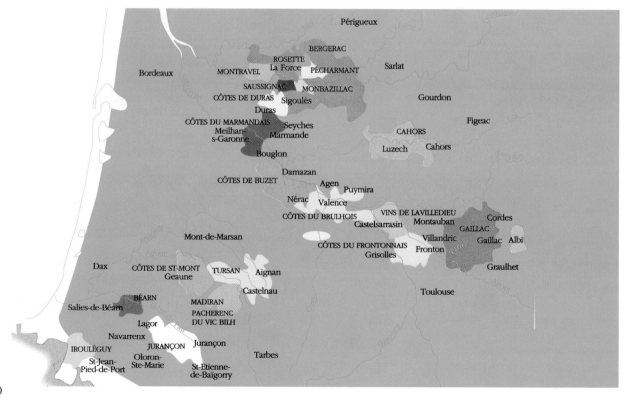

Périgueux

BERGERAC

ROSETTE
La Force

MONTRAVEL
PÉCHARMANT
Sarlat

Bordeaux

SAUSSIGNAC
MONBAZILLAC

CÔTES DE DURAS
Sigoulès
Gourdon

Duras

CÔTES DU MARMANDAIS
Seyches
Figeac

Meilhan-
s-Garonne
Marmande
CAHORS

Bouglon
Luzech
Cahors

Damazan

CÔTES DE BUZET
Agen
Puymira

Nérac
Valence

CÔTES DU BRULHOIS
VINS DE LAVILLEDIEU
Cordes

Castelsarrasin
Montauban
GAILLAC

Mont-de-Marsan
Villandric
Gaillac
Albi

CÔTES DU FRONTONNAIS
Fronton

Grisolles

Dax
Graulhet

CÔTES DE ST-MONT
TURSAN
Aignan

Geaune

Castelnau
Toulouse

BÉARN
MADIRAN

Salies-de-Béarn
PACHERENC
DU VIC BILH

Lagor

Navarrenx

IROULÉGUY
JURANÇON
Jurançon

St-Jean-
Oloron-
Tarbes

Pied-de-Port
Ste-Marie
St-Etienne-
de-Baïgorry

in 1946, comes from the word *pech*, which means top. It is very tannic, powerful and heady, with a minimum of 11 percent alcohol. It has the advantage of developing several qualities right from its youth and does not need to undergo a long aging process. One of the most quoted growths is Château de Tiregand.

MONBAZILLAC

Monbazillac, despite its qualities, does not try to compete with the prestigious syrah wines, even if the locals proudly remember the history of this area, which is also the cradle of noble rot. This wine is a blend of sémillon, sauvignon and muscadelle; it is rich, full bodied and has floral and honey aromas.

ROSETTE

This *appellation*, dating back to 1949, covers six districts on the right bank of the river Dordogne. These wines are sweet or medium sweet and their production is constantly decreasing (17 000 gallons).

SAUSSIGNAC

This white wine *appellation*, very close to Bergerac, can be added to the Côtes de Bergerac *appellation*. It includes the districts of Saussignac, Gageac-et-Rouillac, Monestier and Razac-de-Saussignac. This medium sweet wine is preferably drunk young, although it may keep for about ten years.

MONTRAVEL

This *appellation* covers some dry and fruity white wines made on the right bank of the Dordogne, around the district of Vélines. The *appellations* Côtes-de-Montravel and Haut-Montravel, containing from 12 to 15 percent alcohol, are only produced in some districts and are made exclusively from sauvignon, sévignon and muscadelle.

The whole of this vast region contains about twenty A.O.C.

BERGERACOIS

Bergerac, Côtes de Bergerac, Montravel, Haut-Montravel, Côtes de Montravel, Monbazillac, Pécharmant, Saussignac, Rosette.

AGENAIS

Côtes de Duras, Buzet, Côtes du Marmandais.

PÉRIGORD - QUERCY

The production of these two regions is grouped under Cahors.

ROUERGUE

Marcillac wines.

ALBIGEOIS AND TARN

Gaillac, Gaillac doux, Gaillac-Premières Côtes, sparkling Gaillac.

GASCONY AND PYRENEES

Madiran, Pacherenc du Vic Bilh, Béarn, Jurançon, dry Jurançon, Irouléguy, Côtes du Brublois.

THE SOUTH WEST

CÔTES DU DURAS

The wine made in this region used to be sold as Bordeaux. Then, in 1937, as a consequence of administrative divisions, it was entitled to its own *appellation*. The vine varieties are the same as the ones used to make Bordeaux wines. The reds are rather light, fruity and delicate and should be drunk within the first few years. The dry whites are fresh and fruity and are similar to Burgundy white wines.

BUZET

This new *appellation* was once known as Côtes de Buzet. Vinification was taken up in 1955 by the co-operative of Buzet-sur-Baïse, whose members have limited production in order to improve quality. This gives mainly red wines (95 percent of the total) which are supple and pleasant in their youth and acquire a lot of body and 'heart' after a few years.

CAHORS

This district was finally elevated to full A.O.C. status only as recently as 1971.
The vineyards extend over 8750 acres.
The soil composition is varied: it is made of Kimmeridgian limestone (as in the north of Burgundy) alluvial deposits of the Lot, sand and clay with some traces of iron. This environment produces an extremely black wine, which is powerful and robust.

MARCILLAC

This wine from the Rouergue region takes up 4250 acres among about ten districts, north-west of Rodez. Marcillac was granted its A.O.C. status in 1990. It makes pleasant, colored and rather marked rosés, giving off an agreeable raspberry perfume.

GAILLAC

An A.O.C. since 1938, this wine zone has shrunk considerably and only about twenty districts are now devoted to production, which is nevertheless nearly 2.6 million gallons a year and includes a wide range of vine varieties. Dry white wines are produced on granite soil and are lively, clear, nervy and fruity. The right bank of the river Tarn is rich in limestone and yields a generous and round sweet white wine. The reds are brilliant, tannic, round and full bodied and reach maturity quite rapidly. The rosés are fresh, fruity and lively.

CÔTES DU FRONTONNAIS

This *appellation*, created in February 1975, covers over 4250 acres and produces 2.1 million gallons a year.

PACHERENC DU VIC BILH MADIRAN

In 1975, this region was awarded two *appellations*: a red wine - Madiran - and a white one, Pacherenc du Vic Bilh.

The production of the first is over 1.3 million gallons while the second one totals a much smaller 130 000. Pacherenc du Vic Bilh is a slightly robust wine, rather dry and fruity, with a subtle and tender bouquet. Madiran, on the other hand, is robust, tannic to the point of becoming nearly black and 'firm', in the sense that it only acquires its qualities after a long period of aging.

JURANÇON

Jurançon is known for its sweet white wine, but there is also a dry version. This is a very fresh, lively and generous wine, it is long and has an aroma of acacia and broom. It represents the bulk of the production of the *appellation*. After vinification, Jurançon is kept in barrels for four years before being bottled; it contains at least 12.5 percent alcohol.

WHICH CHEESE?

CANTAL
FOURME
MAROILLES
PICODON
ROQUEFORT
OSSAU-IRRATY
BLEU DES CAUSSES
BLEU D'AUVERGNE

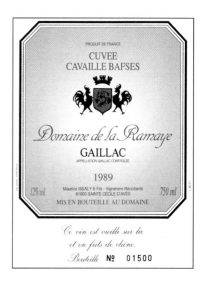

CHARACTERISTICS

Monbazillac and Jurançon are made from grapes harvested over successive pickings once the berries reach over-ripening, that is to say when they are coated with noble rot.

53

THE LOIRE VALLEY

SANCERRE

This wine with a fine greenish golden color, a gunflint aroma and a legendary dryness and freshness makes an unrivalled gastronomic match with Crottin de Chavignol cheese. The *appellation* area com-

mas, are very concentrated, and sturdy. Their remarkable sweet twang is magnificent when matched with fresh or dry little goat cheeses. This cheese has an A.O.C. status too, awarded in 1976.

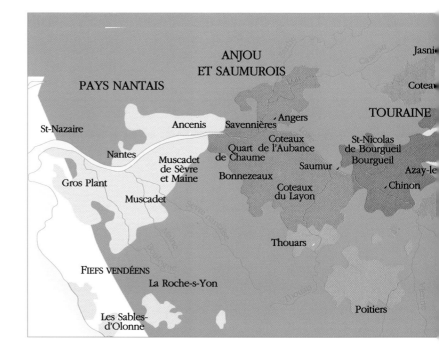

prises ten villages (Baunay, Bué, Crézancy, Menetou-Râtel, Ménétreol, Montigny Thanvenay, Veaugne, Vigny, Vinon) with three renowned growths.

These wines have very fine aro-

VOUVRAY

This prestigious vineyard of about 4500 acres sprawls on the northern bank of the Loire, uphill from Tours, at the very entrance to the town of Vouvray itself.

Vouvray is made exclusively from a grape called pineau de la Loire or chenin. Here, the vine variety grows on a large base of *tuffeau* (a calcareous rock, typical of the region) on a clay-silica or clay-pebble flint-rich soil and yields the most remarkable white wine variety of the whole valley. Vouvray dry whites are supple, tender, fruity and sit on the palate somewhat in their youth. They normally reach full maturity after about ten years of aging.

still or fizzy and is made exclusively from chenin grapes.

TOURAINE - AMBOISE

This 550-acre vineyard dominates the royal castle of Amboise. It is mostly famous for its white wines, which are particularly fresh, fruity and light.
The cot, cabernet and gamay varieties grow well on this site.

WHICH CHEESE?

BRIE DE MEAUX
CROTTIN DE CHAVIGNOL
POULIGNY-SAINT-PIERRE
SELLES SUR CHER

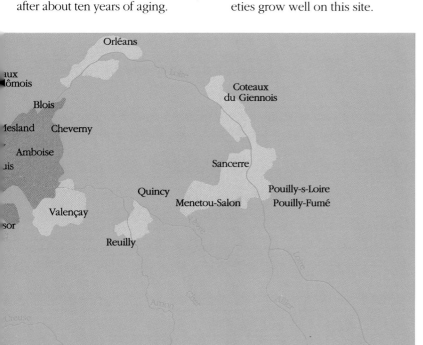

MONTLOUIS

This 750-acre vineyard lies in the region between the Loire and the Cher rivers stretching down to Tussault, a few miles from Amboise. This varietal wine can be

TOURAINE - CHEVERNY

This *appellation* includes some still red and white wines, together with fizzy wines obtained from the blending of nineteen different grape varieties.

THE LOIRE VALLEY

GRAPE VARIETIES

FOR RED WINES
GROLLEAU
CABERNET FRANC
CABERNET SAUVIGNON
GAMAY
COT

FOR WHITE WINES
CHENIN
MUSCADET OR MELON
FOLLE BLANCHE
SAUVIGNON
CHASSELAS

CHINON

If you follow the river Vienne upstream, in the footsteps of Joan of Arc, you will see Rivière, Sazilly, Tavant, Ile-Bouchard and Crouzille, all inland and on the hillsides of the Chinon district, along the regional highway 21. Further on, you will come across Cravant-les-Coteaux, Pauzoult and Cigré, all villages cherished by Rabelais.

These villages make wines with delicate perfumes of violet combined with wild strawberry, whose color is pure ruby. They are pleasant and supple, permanently evoking their soil through a strong taste of humus and truffle. As in the case of Bourgueil, an experienced palate would be able to distinguish between a wine made on terraces and one made on the hillsides. There, the soil is a combination of clay and limestone or clay and silica and produces very sturdy and powerful wines, well suited for the long term. Wines made on terraces grow on a gravely and sandy soil, thirty-three feet below sea level; they are finer, more fruity and must be drunk soon.

BOURGUEIL-SAINT-NICOLAS-DE-BOURGUEIL

If you want to get from Tours to Bourgueil, take the *route nationale* 152 highway, built on the rise of the river. After Langeais, take the *route départementale* 35. This is the wine route, which takes you through a whole host of tiny little zones that also form *appellation* areas. Your only guide will be the names of the districts: Saint-Nicolas, Saint-Patrice, Ingrande-de-Touraine, Restigné, Berrais, La Chapelle, Chouzé-sur-Loire and - right to the west - Bourgueil.

These two vineyards used to be under the authority of the Anjou region and sprawl over 9.5 miles perpendicular to the Loire river, from Saint-Patrice to Montsoreau. Like in Chinon, the vines grow mainly on a vast alluvial terrace on the banks of the Loire and produce a 'gravely wine', which is quickly made, finer and more fruity than the ones growing on *tuffeau*.

The latter vineyards can be found in the north, at Bourgueil and Saint-Nicolas-de-Bourgueil. These wines are harder in their youth than their companions. However, they can improve dramatically after a few years of aging.

The 4200-acre extension of both *appellations*, like the rest of the region, is dominated by the cabernet franc (or breton) variety of grape, although a little cabernet sauvignon is still permitted.

Opposite and below, the Saumur vineyard.

COTEAUX DU LAYON

It is one of the most prestigious *appellations* of Anjou. Its 5000 acres stretch down 50 miles, all along the banks of the Layon - a tributary of the Loire - from its source at Cléré-sur-Layon to its mouth at Chalonnes, a port built by the Dutch in the 18th century. This valley seems to be made specially for chenin grapes. The curve of the Layon has its own distinctive environmental character. The best sites are on the right bank, from Concourson to Rochefort-sur-Loire, producing a cascade of long-lived wines with an exceptional aromatic complexity. Seven of the 25 districts form the Coteaux du Layon-Villages *appellation*, which gives great sweet or viscous white wines with delicate smells of honey and quince and a sumptuous greenish gold color. The districts in question are: Beaulieu, Faye-d'Anjou, Rablay, Saint-Lambert, Saint-Aubin, Rochefort-sur-Loire and the small village of Chaume.

CHARACTERISTICS

Chinon and Bourgueil are both made from cabernet franc. Chinon is lighter than Bourgueil and is drunk faster, although it keeps longer.

57

THE LOIRE VALLEY

GRAPE VARIETIES

CHENIN
MUSCADET OR MELON
FOLLE BLANCHE
SAUVIGNON
CHASSELAS

Vineyards planted with muscadet stretch over a large, flat area of 42 000 acres, rolling along the river Loire upstream from Nantes and to the west until it reaches the sea. The eastern border is marked by the Maine-et-Loire region to the east and Vendée to the south, just after the Loire-Atlantique district. On this vast territory dominated by muscadet, only 7500 acres are allocated to the training of Gros Plant *appellations*. Muscadet grapes are simple and elegant, with a very pale, green-hued golden color and no more than 12 percent alcohol to preserve freshness; they are used to produce a world famous wine, which is best grown in this region.

MUSCADET SUR LIE

The area around Nantes has the earliest harvest in France.
Grapes could follow the normal vinification procedures used for white wines. However, two thirds of Muscadet wines and an increasing proportion of Gros Plant is labelled 'stored on lees (*sur lie*) until bottling', which happens in June and is done without previous racking, but simply by exploiting gravity. The wine undergoes minimum stirring and therefore keeps part of its natural carbon dioxide. This results in a slight fizziness (*perlant*) which distinguishes Muscadet sur Lie as soon as the bottle is opened. Good vintages of Muscadet under-

going proper vinification make excellent wines, with a fine bouquet, a light, virtually airy structure and slight acidity. Their freshness makes them one of the most popular wines of France.

MUSCADET DE SÈVRE-ET-MAINE

Two thirds of all Muscadet wine come from this area where the rivers Sèvre and Maine join.
The best vineyards are concentrated here, on a rather granite terrain. The town of Vallet, with its 5500-acre vineyards, is regarded as the capital of Muscadet.

MUSCADET DES COTEAUX DE LA LOIRE

This *appellation* extends around Ancenis on both banks of the Loire. Muscadet grapes, which account for about 10 percent of the total, give more solid and robust wines than those produced in Sèvre-et-Maine and some of them have an aroma of gunflint.

COTEAUX D'ANCENIS

At the very tip of Pays Nantais, just before the Anjou region, this 1000-acre vineyard makes mainly reds and rosés from gamay noir à jus blanc. These are pleasant and fruity wines and represent 80 percent of total production. The whites, trained closer to the Anjou region, are made from chenin. Here, wine producers are required to specify the name of the grape variety on the label.

MUSCADET

This *appellation* covers the town of Retz, bastion of the famous Gilles de Rais, martial of France and friend of Joan of Arc. The zone sprawls down to encroach on the Vendée district. The Grandlieu lake, an outstanding marshy area housing over 220 different species of birds, lies at the heart of this vast territory.

Muscadet, a rather rustic wine, is lively, fresh and fruity. It should be drunk young, right from the following springtime.

GROS PLANT DU PAYS NANTAIS

This *appellation* is cut into a wide, muscat-dominated region. It has to make do with the sandy and gravely soil of the Loire-Atlantique region and with the land surrounding the Grandlieu lake. Its only grape variety is gros plant, otherwise known as follie blanche. This 7500-acre zone produces a definitely coarser and greener wine than Muscadet.

WHICH CHEESE?

CROTTIN DE CHAVIGNOL
CHABICHOU
POULIGNY-SAINT-PIERRE
SELLES SUR CHER
SAINTE-MAURE

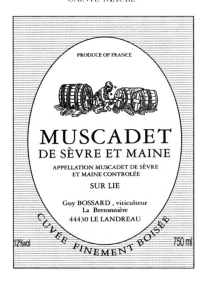

CHARACTERISTICS

Muscadet wines are light, supple and fruity and are best drunk young. They have a limpid color and their nose often releases sweet floral or even fruity aromas.

Their impact on the palate is flattering and persistent, ending in a long, pleasantly harmonious finish.

59

THE JURA

At the end of the 19th century, in this region rich in old vine varieties, about forty different grapes were regularly used. In modern Jura, only five are allowed an A.O.C. status. As far as reds are concerned, the poulsard, a plant originating in this region, represents 20 percent of the overall vine-growing area. It owes its name to the *pelouse*, a type of edible wild berry. The grapes develop big berries and make claret-style reds. Trousseau, another local red grape variety, is the rarest of the region. It is planted on a mere 5 percent of the whole vineyard area. Its berries make a densely colored red wine, giving it body and good behavior through the aging process. Pinot noir is used to enhance both the color and the body of poulsard.

As for the white wines, chardonnay, also known as melon d'Arbois, is the dominant grape (45 percent). It gives a dry and fruity wine. The savagnin variety, also called naturé, is trained on wild vineyards cultivated by the nuns at Château-Chalon. Savagnin is usually blended with chardonnay.

When not blended, it becomes yellow wine after aging in barrels.

Jura's white wines (such as the Côtes du Jura, Arbois and Étoile *appellations*) are usually stored in oak barrels for two to three years; there, they acquire a pleasant bouquet of grilled nuts (hazelnuts and almonds).

These wines are long-lived, dry and fruity on the palate, with a nose strongly evoking their vineyards of origin and full bodied.

Red and rosé wines (as in the Côtes du Jura and Arbois *appellations*) display aromas of flowers and small fruit. They are made either from poulsard or trousseau. The first has a slightly pink color, which turns into reddish brown with aging. The latter is red and more powerful and sturdy.

The most characteristic products are *vins de paille* (straw wines) and yellow wines.

VIN DE PAILLE (STRAW WINE)

This is an harmonious mix of grapes from various varieties such as savagnin, trousseau, chardonnay, poulsard. Bunches are left on straw, clay, or simply suspended for two to three months, until they are over-ripe. Pressing is followed by a lengthy fermentation, which may last from one to two years and produces a sugar-rich wine with between 14.5 and 17 percent alcohol. Finally, once it is put in barrels, it is left to age for three years before being bottled.

VIN JAUNE (YELLOW WINE)

Yellow wine is made exclusively from savagnin grapes. After several months of fermentation, it is racked and stored in oak barrels, where it is left to age for at least six years, without further topping up or racking. The film of yeast which forms on the surface serves as a protection from rapid oxidation. The wine slowly changes color and acquires a 'taste of yellow'.

The *clavelin*, a special bottle used for this wine, has a capacity of 1.09 pints, which corresponds to the amount of wine left from three quarters of a pint after the losses due to evaporation over six years of aging. The result of this whole process is a golden, very aromatic wine, which is long on the palate and has hints of green nuts, almonds and grilled hazelnuts.

WHICH CHEESE?

SAINT-NECTAIRE
FOURME

The most popular appellations *are:* Côtes du Jura, Arbois, Arbois-Pupillin, sparkling Arbois, Château-Chalon, L'Étoile, sparkling Étoile, Macvin.

The Jura also includes two unusual and very tasty appellations: vin de paille *and* vin jaune.

CHARACTERISTICS

Both vin de paille *and* yellow wine *are rare and expensive. They are produced in small quantities and undergo a long and difficult vinification process. Savagnin, the only grape making yellow wine, is harvested late, usually after the first snow.*
The wine-making procedures for these wines are similar to those used for Sherry, in Spain.

61

SAVOY

The Savoy region is planted with several famous vines such as chasselas, gamay, pinot and a host of indigenous varieties such as bergeron - grown in Chignin - roussette, gringet, molette, douce noire (or montmélian plant), persan and many more.

Ripaille, which was already devoted to wine-growing in Roman times, at the end of the 13th century was a popular hunting venue.

Despite various transformations during the 19th century, its fortress is still imposing, surrounded by a 120-acre park and a 37-acre wine *appellation.* Marin, near Thonon, produces a fresh and fruity A.O.C. white wine on a 60-acre vineyard.

The Ayze vineyards, near Bonneville, at the foot of the Mole mountain, date back to the 13th century; references to them appear as early as in the writings of St. Francis of Sales.

This 75-acre zone produces sparkling wines obtained through the traditional technique. The grapes used are the roussette of ayze and gringet (a kind of gewürztraminer).

In the 17th century, the picturesque hamlet of Frangy was involved in the wine trade with Switzerland.

Today, a syndicate gathers the producers of twelve districts. It makes a delicate and distinguished roussette de Savoy wine, a fruity gamay, a firm yet perfumed mondeuse and lively Savoy rosés. The Seyssel vineyard became an A.O.C. in 1942; it devotes 170 acres to the production of full-bodied, tender, supple and robust white wines, made from roussette (also known as altesse) and molette grapes. In the remaining 25 acres, gamay and mondeuse are grown to produce red wine.

Ruffieux lies at the heart of the Chautagne wine-growing area. It

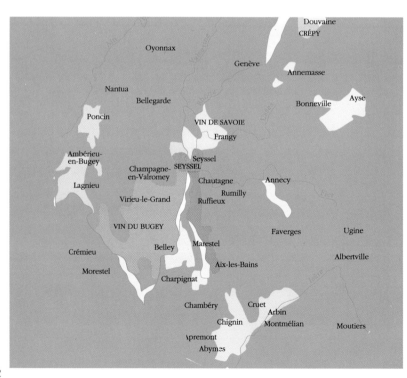

gathers the production of more than 200 estates, covering the districts of Motz, Serrières and Chindrieux. In the 18th century, it used to be the favourite wine at the court of Sardinia. At present, production is made up of 30 percent white wines (of which 20 percent slightly sparkling jacquère and 10 percent slightly sparkling roussette and aligoté) and 70 percent of reds, of which gamay accounts for 45 percent and both pinot and mondeuse account for 12.5 percent. These three red varieties are also successfully mixed to give Chautagnard, the latest local blend.

VINS DE BUGEY

These wines are less famous than their Savoy counterparts, but they are just as old. Under the influence of the Roman Gauls first and then of the monks, their reputation spread. Whites are made from the usual varieties of roussanne, chardonnay, jacquère, aligoté, white mondeuse and the exclusively local molette. They are called Roussette de Bugey, of which Montagnieu is the most renowned, and Bugey Sparkling Wine. They are very aromatic and racy.

Bugey reds, on the other hand, are produced from gamay, pinot noir, poulsard and mondeuse. Their qualities depend very much upon their origin. They can be robust if they are made from mondeuse, fine and perfumed if they are made from pinot (as with Manicle) and supple and fruity if they are gamay. A blend of gamay and poulsard produces Cerdon rosé, a lightly sparkling wine.

WHICH CHEESE?

ABONDANCE
COMTÉ
BEAUFORT

VINS DE SAVOIE

Savoy wines usually mention on the label the dominant grape variety. However, the appellation *comprises various growths: Ripaille, Marignan, Abymes, Apremont, Saint-Jeoire-Prieuré, Chignin, Chignin-Bergeron, Montmélian, Arbois, Cruet, Saint-Jean-de-la-Porte, Sainte-Marie-d'Allaix, Ayze, Roussette de Savoie, Seyssel, sparkling Seyssel and Crépy.*

VINS DU BUGEY

As for all Savoy wines, Bugey wines bear the name of the grapes used (pinot, gamay...). In five cases, the name of the vineyard is suffixed: Virieule-Grand, Maride, Maduraz, Montagnieu, Cerdon.

ROUSSETTE DU BUGEY

Within the regional appellation*, these white wines may come from six vineyards: Lagnieu, Montagnieu, Virieu-le-Grand, Arbigneu, Anglefort and Chanay.*

ALSACE

Alsace wines are all A.O.C. and are divided into four big appella-tions.

THE REGIONAL APPELLATION ALSACE OR VINS D'ALSACE

It is normally appended to the name of the grape variety used, like riesling or muscat.

THE VINS D'ALSACE APPELLATION

These Grands Crus are made from four noble vine varieties (gewürztraminer, riesling, pinot gris and muscat) and are pro-duced in limited zones.

THE COMMUNAL AND SINGLE-VINEYARD APPELLATIONS

About fifty wines are allowed to mention their vineyard of origin, whose name is added to the other wording, like in Sporen at Riquewihr, Schlossberg at Wettol-sheim, Wiebelsberg at Andlau.

THE CRÉMANT D'ALSACE APPELLATION

These sparkling wines are made from white grapes and produced following the traditional sparkling wine-making method. Peculiarities: Edelzwicker is a white wine made from a blend of noble vine varieties.

Did they make wine in Alsace be-fore Roman times? This is a much debated question. Anyway, it has now been established that the Ro-mans first introduced wine-grow-ing in this region, changing agri-cultural structures and co-operat-ing with the Gauls.

During the Middle Ages, Alsace was renowned for its wines. They were exported to Cologne and subsequently shipped to Scandi-navia and England. Wine-growing in Alsace thrived from the 3rd to the 16th century. The Thirty-Year War, which placed much of the re-gion under French rule, ruined both vineyards and trade. New vines were therefore planted. The 18th century was quite gloomy, al-though Alsace wines were all the fashion in Austria and Switzerland. After the French Revolution, vine-yards were broken up into plots, which brought many wine-grow-ers to privilege high-yielding vine varieties. However, the little pros-perity they enjoyed during the 19th century did not last very long. In 1871 Alsace was annexed by

Germany, which adopted policies to prevent these wines from com-peting with German ones. Local wine-makers were thus encour-aged to produce cheap wines. To make things worse, an outbreak of phylloxera brought producers to plant hybrids, which resisted the parasite but gave mediocre results. In 1918, Alsace returned to French rule. It was simply disas-trous for local growers, who could not find buyers for their wines. The only remedy was to adopt a quality-oriented policy, which also meant switching to other vine varieties.

Wine-growers got down to the task and their products slowly re-covered their long lost reputation. These efforts were ratified by a de-cree on 2 November 1945 which defined the status of Alsace wines. After a few spells of bad luck, Al-sace producers were given a quasi monopoly over the *flûte*, a superb, easily recognisable tall bottle. On the other hand, they had to wait until 1962 before their wines were awarded A.O.C. status.

NOBLE VINE VARIETIES

GEWÜRZTRAMINER

Origin: traminer or savagnin rosé variety.
Quality: early ripening, medium yields.
Picking: at ripening.
Bouquet: intense, displaying many nuances and floral aromas.
Taste: Full bodied and robust.

RIESLING

Origin: Orléans region.
Quality: late ripening, high yields.
Picking: late.
Bouquet: elegant, fruity and delicate
Taste: dry, slightly acid.

MUSCAT

Origin: known in Alsace since 1523.
Varieties: Pink Muscat of Alsace and White Muscat-Ottonel.
Quality: Pink Muscat is a late-ripening vine, unlike Muscat-Ottonel.
Bouquet: delicate and very fruity.
Taste: musky, with a marked grapey taste.

TOKAY OR PINOT GRIS

Origin: Burgundy.
Quality: early ripening, low yields.
Picking: at ripening.
Bouquet: rich and fresh.
Taste: heady, powerful, meaty, robust and dry, with a touch of mellow.

ALSACE

Alsace's yearly production is in the order of 2.6 million gallons of A.O.C. wine, 93 percent of which is white and 7 percent reds and

Above, the village of Riquewihr.

rosés. Even the grumpiest walker would succumb to the charms of this region. The rounded hills, the half-timbered houses with flowers overflowing from their windows, the vineyards and the orchards all conjure up an outstanding canvas.

It would be tedious to list the sixty landmarks to be found along Alsace's wine route. What follows is therefore only a selection, going from north to south.

Nordheim, built on a mound halfway between Strasbourg and Saverne, is a beautiful start to the wine route, offering a panoramic view over the Alsatian plain.

The small village of Bergbieten paradoxically makes a great growth, the local Riesling, also called Altenberg.

Soultz-les-Bains marks the beginning of the vineyards belonging to the lower Rhine region proper. Molsheim, where Bugatti cars used to be made, is surrounded by vineyards and houses a regional museum. The nests of the cranes perching on the rooftops catch the tourist's attention when walking around the town.

Obernai still preserves sites of great historical interest, superb monuments dating back to the Middle Ages and the Renaissance, like the Town Hall, the Corn Exchange and the chapel tower. It also houses a big brewery, which is a sign of the town's vine-growing dedication. The near hillsides of Schenkenberg and Nationalberg produce an excellent Gewürztraminer. Ottrott, at the foot of mount Odile, makes the distinctive Roter Ottroter, a pinot noir which is one of Alsace's oldest red wines. Heiligenstein pleases the eye as well as the palate. There, one can find the klevner growth, for which they use a vine imported from Italy in the 18th century, as well as a beautiful fountain and a stunning view over the Alsace plain.

Alsace wines are largely dry and very shady whites. However, there are also excellent red wines, made from Burgundy pinot noir.

GEWÜRZTRAMINER

It is the most distinctive of Alsace's vine varieties, due to its spicy and musky aromas. It gives dry or sparkling wines with an exceptional fruity bouquet.

RIESLING

This small-berried, low-yielding variety is definitely the most noble of the region. It gives dry and racy wines, with a pale green color and a subtle and delicate perfume.

PINOT GRIS

This too is a low-yielding vine. It used to be known as tokay and gives powerful and heady wines which are widely appreciated locally.

MUSCAT

Alsace Muscat is a rare example of this variety making a dry white. This wine, with a subtle and fruity perfume, is often recommended as an aperitif.

WHICH CHEESE?

MUNSTER

The village of Kayserberger.

CHARACTERISTICS

Alsatian wines have a superb color, they are quite typical and very harmonious to the nose.
Light and tender in the mouth and persistent on the palate, they possess an alluring aromatic intensity.

67

CHAMPAGNE

GRAPE VARIETIES

CHARDONNAY
PINOT NOIR
PINOT MEUNIER

Champagne vineyards sprawl over several regions: Marne, Aube, Aisne, Haute-Marne and Seine-et-Marne. They are divided into four main areas: the Reims mountain,

the Marne valley, the Côte des Blancs and the Aube vineyards. This 87 000-acre extension is planted with pinot meunier (45 percent), pinot noir (30 percent) and

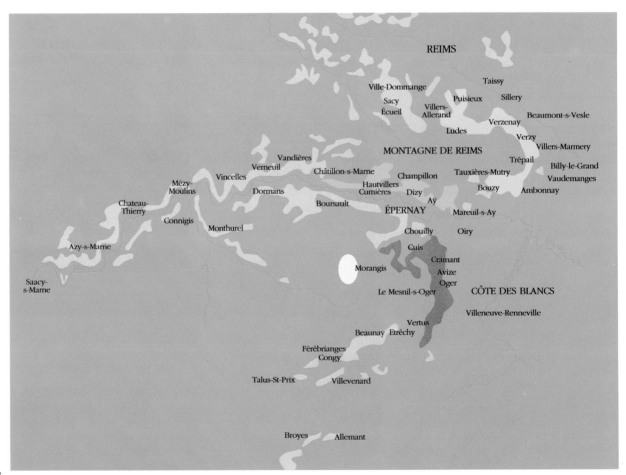

REIMS

Ville-Dommange
Sacy
Écueil
Villers-Allerand
Puisieux
Taissy
Sillery
Beaumont-s-Vesle
Verzenay
Ludes
Verzy
Villers-Marmery

MONTAGNE DE REIMS

Vandières
Verneuil
Vincelles
Châtillon-s-Marne
Champillon
Tauxières-Mutry
Trépail
Billy-le-Grand
Vaudemanges
Mézy-Moulins
Dormans
Hautvillers
Cumières
Dizy
Bouzy
Ambonnay
Chateau-Thierry
Boursault
Aÿ
ÉPERNAY
Mareuil-s-Ay
Connigis
Monthurel
Chouilly
Oiry
Azy-s-Marne
Cuis
Morangis
Cramant
Avize
Oger
Saacy-s-Marne
Le Mesnil-s-Oger
CÔTE DES BLANCS
Villeneuve-Renneville
Vertus
Beaunay Etréchy
Férébrianges
Congy
Talus-St-Prix
Villevenard
Broyes
Allemant

chardonnay (25 percent).

The chalky soil favors the drainage of excess water, and also keeps and then releases humidity and the heat of the sun. This endows Champagne wines with finesse and lightness.

Vinification is carried out according to the special *méthode champenoise*, the traditional sparkling wine-making process. Several geological discoveries trace the origins of the first vines of this area to the Tertiary period. Champagne wines were first annexed to the Ile-de-France region and were defined *vins français* or *vins de France* (French wines' or 'Wines from France'). Changes in vinification, which produced grey and then white wines, led to a change in the *appellation*. In 1936, the Champagne A.O.C. was created. These wines are classified differently according to wine blends and dosage. They can be either traditional, resulting from a blend of several vintages; single-vintage (a blend of the produce of the same vintage); *blanc de blanc* (made exclusively from white grapes); *cuvée spéciale*, or special blend, for which each wine-maker has their own recipe; rosé - or pink - champagne, made by adding a little Champagne red wine to the blend. It is the amount of expedition liquor added that classifies these wines into: brut, extra dry, sec, demisec and rich, or *doux*. Another *appellation* is Crémant, comprising slightly less fizzy wines.

THE GRANDS CRUS

According to the quality of both grapes and vineyards, a scale has been created going from 80 percent to 100 percent. This scale also determines the selling price of the grapes. At the very top of the list, there are seventeen Grands Crus. *These are produced in the Marne region, in the region of the Reims Great Mountain and on the Côte des Blancs.*

PREMIERS CRUS

In the 90 to 99 percent section of the scale there are forty-four Premiers Crus, *produced between the Reims Small Mountain, the Marne valley around Aÿ and south of the Côte des Blancs.*

BLANC DE BLANCS CHAMPAGNE

This is a very fine and fruity varietal wine, made exclusively from chardonnay grapes. Blanc de Noirs champagne, on the other hand, is made from white-juiced black grapes (pinot noir and pinot meunier).

ROSÉ CHAMPAGNE

This drink gets its color through the addition of a small proportion of red wine made on the Champagne escarpments.

COTEAUX CHAMPENOIS

They are still, simple and fruity wines. The best one is undoubtedly red Bouzy.

ROSÉ DE RICEYS

This small appellation lies on the border with Burgundy.

CHAMPAGNE

Coteaux Champenois wines (A.O.C. in 1974) are still whites, reds, or rosés which are picked and produced in this region.

Wines like the red Bouzy, with a raspberry taste and a pleasant violet bouquet, are supple and slightly colored. In their best vintages, they can be robust and long-lived.

Rosés de Ricey, made from pinot noir grapes, possess amazing qualities, borrowed from both Champagne and Burgundy wines.

The only problem is that they are extremely rare. Indeed, only a few wine-growers, the so-called *récoltants manipulants* (estate bottlers) make their own wine. The rest sell their grapes in bulk either to co-operatives or to big wine merchants, some of which do not even own a vineyard.

VALLÉE DE LA MARNE

Boursault brings back the crazy times of the French *Belle Époque* period, through the beautiful *château* that Mme Cliquot had built in 1948 for her daughter and her son-in-law, Louis de Chevigné. Hautvillers houses an abbey of the same name, which now belongs to the Moët and Chandon label. This village gives a warm tribute to Dom Pérignon, the 'inventor' of

champagne, a monk who gave prestige to this naturally fermenting wine.

MONTAGNE DE REIMS

This area covers the mountain itself, the smaller mountain of Reims and the hills of Bouzy.

The royal city of Reims is the capital of champagne. Its ancient Roman chalk caves, after having been long exploited, were turned into cellars. A compulsory visit should be paid to the Pommery caves, running underground for 11 miles and on which stand Elizabethan-style buildings dating back to 1878.

Low-relief sculptures by Navlet (1888) can also be admired here, together with a 18 500 gallon cask (*foudre*), whose base was sculpted by Émile Gallé.

Bouzy is the main producer of Champagne great red wines, but, more importantly, it is a Champagne *Premier Cru*.

The other districts making red wines are: Ambonnay, Aÿ, Mareuil, Tours-sur-Marne, Chigny-les-Roses, Rilly-la-Montagne, Jouy-les-Reims, Cumières and Vertus.

The estate of Louvois, named after a minister of King Louis XIV, appears a humbler copy of Versailles. The Laurent-Perrier label bought it

in 1989. Aÿ houses some great labels such as Alaya, Bollinger, Deutz and Gosset.

CÔTES DES BLANCS

Épernay, together with Reims, houses the majority of great winemakers. Millions of bottles lie in hundreds of miles of underground cellars.

It is a good place to find out about vinification techniques and taste vintages from different labels.

A major feature is the *foudre* of Mercier, which has a capacity corresponding to 215 000 bottles. It took about thirty years to build and was the main attraction of the 1889 Universal Exhibition.

Cramant is a wine-growing village producing a renowned growth. Another important winegrowing centre is Vertus, a small medieval village surrounded by ramparts.

RICEY WINES

This region on the border with Burgundy makes very good dry rosés, whose production never exceeds 15 600 gallons.

WHICH CHEESE?

LANGRES
CHAOURCE

Opposite and above, harvesting at Veuve-Cliquot.

CHARACTERISTICS

In the Champagne region, grapes are picked at ripening, although special care is taken to avoid over-ripening, which could affect perfume. Berries are handled cautiously before the bunches are trimmed. Finally, pressing takes place in special presses.

71

BIBLIOGRAPHY

L'Atlas des vins de France. Frenand Woutaz. (Ed. Jean-Pierre de Monza).

La cote des vins 1993-1994. Arthur Choko. 1992 (Ed. de l'Amateur).

La dégustation. Steven Spurrier et Michel Dovaz. Collection Académie du vin (Bordas).

Dictionnaire des vins. Dr. Gérard Debuigne. Collection Références. 1985 (Larousse).

Dijon, la route des vins. Pays de France. Mars-Avril 1993 (Ed. Mondiales).

Encyclopédie des vins et alcools. Alexis Lichine. Collection Bouquins (Robert Laffont).

Le Guide des vins de Bourgogne. Guy Renvoisé. (Solarama).

Le Guide des vins de Champagne. Guy Renvoisé. 1983 (Solarama).

Guide de vins. Que choisir Pratique (UFC).

Histoire du vin. Jean-François Gautier. Collection Que sais-je? (PUF).

Le Livre pratique des vins. Michel Dovaz. (De Vecchi poche).

Nouveau Larousse des vins. Dr. Gérard Debuigne. 1979. (Larousse).

Soignez-vous par le vin. Dr. E.A. Maury (Marabout).

Sur les chemins des vignobles de France. (Sélection du Reader's Digest).

Sur les routes des vins de France. Alexis Lichine. 1986 (Robert Laffont).

France. Collection Guides bleus. 1990 (Hachette).

Terroirs et vins de France: Sous la direction de Charles Pomerol. (Editions du BRGM).

La Vigne et le vin. Hors série «Science et Vie». Septembre 1986.

Le Vignoble savoyard et ses vins. Roger Girel. 1985 (Ed. Glénat).

Le Vin d'Arbois. 1989 par le Commandant G. Grand. 1989.

Le vin mode d'emploi. Hugh Johnson. 1985. (Ed. Flammarion).

Les vins de Bourgogne. Pierre Poupon et Pierre Forgeot. 1969 (PUF).

PHOTOGRAPHS

J Bravo: pages 47,60,61.

A.N.A. Agency:

R. Nourry: page 61 - J. Rey: page 40 - Henneghien: pages 33, 34 - Durazzo: page 44 - Thomas: page 47.

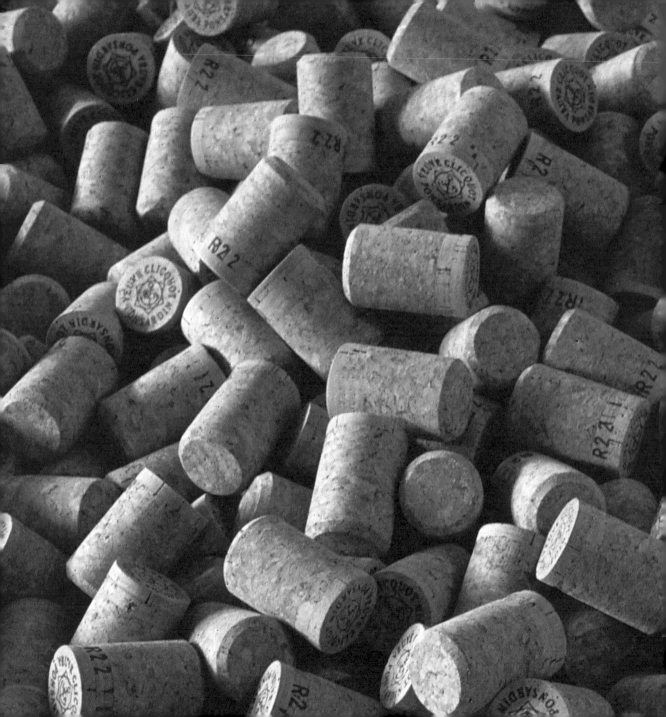